SHEPHERD'S NOTES

Shepherd's Notes Titles Available

SHEPHERD'S NOTES COMMENTARY SERIES

Old Testament

9-780-805-490-282 Genesis
9-780-805-490-565 Exodus
9-780-805-490-695 Leviticus, Numbers
9-780-805-490-275 Deuteronomy
9-780-805-490-589 Joshua, Judges
9-780-805-490-572 Ruth, Esther
9-780-805-490-633 1 & 2 Samuel
9-780-805-490-077 1 & 2 Kings
9-780-805-490-649 1 & 2 Chronicles
9-780-805-491-944 Ezra, Nehemiah
9-780-805-490-060 Job
9-780-805-493-399 Psalms 1-50

9-780-805-493-405 Psalms 51-100
9-780-805-493-412 Psalms 101-150
9-780-805-490-169 Proverbs
9-780-805-490-596 Ecclesiastes, Song of
      Solomon
9-780-805-491-975 Isaiah
9-780-805-490-701 Jeremiah, Lamentations
9-780-805-490-787 Ezekiel
9-780-805-490-152 Daniel
9-780-805-493-269 Hosea, Obadiah
9-780-805-493-344 Jonah, Zephaniah
9-780-805-490-657 Haggai, Malachi

New Testament

9-781-558-196-889 Matthew
9-780-805-490-718 Mark
9-780-805-490-046 Luke
9-781-558-196-933 John
9-781-558-196-919 Acts
9-780-805-490-053 Romans
9-780-805-493-252 1 Corinthians
9-780-805-493-351 2 Corinthians
9-781-558-196-902 Galatians
9-780-805-493-276 Ephesians

9-781-558-196-896 Philippians, Colossians,
      Philemon
9-780-805-490-008 1 & 2 Thessalonians
9-781-558-196-926 1 & 2 Timothy, Titus
9-780-805-493-368 Hebrews
9-780-805-490-183 James
9-780-805-490-190 1 & 2 Peter & Jude
9-780-805-492-149 1, 2 & 3 John
9-780-805-490-176 Revelation

SHEPHERD'S NOTES CHRISTIAN CLASSICS

9-780-805-493-474 *Mere Christianity,*
      C. S. Lewis
9-780-805-493-535 *The Problem of Pain/*
      A Grief Observed,
      C. S. Lewis
9-780-805-491-999 *The Confessions,*
      Augustine
9-780-805-492-002 *Calvin's Institutes*
9-780-805-493-948 *Miracles,* C. S. Lewis

9-780-805-491-968 *Lectures to My Students,*
      Charles Haddon
      Spurgeon
9-780-805-492-200 *The Writings of Justin*
      Martyr
9-780-805-493-450 *The City of God,*
      Augustine
9-780-805-491-982 *The Cost of Discipleship,*
      Bonhoeffer

SHEPHERD'S NOTES — BIBLE SUMMARY SERIES

9-780-805-493-771 Old Testament
9-780-805-493-788 New Testament

9-780-805-493-849 Life & Teachings of Jesus
9-780-805-493-856 Life & Letters of Paul

SHEPHERD'S NOTES

Bible Summary Series

The
New Testament

HOLMAN
REFERENCE

NASHVILLE, TENNESSEE

Shepherd's Notes—New Testament
© 2000
by B&H Publishing Group
Nashville, Tennessee
All rights reserved
Printed in the United States of America

978-0-8054-9378-8
Dewey Decimal Classification: 225.6
Subject Heading: Bible. N.T.
Library of Congress Card Catalog Number: 99-054017

Library of Congress Cataloging-in-Publication Data

Gould, Dana, 1951–
    New Testament / by Dana Gould.
        p. cm.   — (Shepherd's notes.)
    Includes bibliographical references.
    ISBN 0–8054–9378–6
    1. Bible. N.T.—Study and teaching.   I. Title. II. Series.
    BS2330.2.G65 2000
    225.6'1—dc21   99–054017
                                                                  CIP

4 5 6 7 8 9 10   16 15 14 13 12

CONTENTS

Dear Reader:

Shepherd's Notes are now available on every book in the Bible. In addition, we are pleased to provide a number of volumes in what we call **The Bible Summary Series**. This series will give you a perspective on various parts of the Bible that you wouldn't get by focusing on a book at time. These volumes include *Old Testament, New Testament, Life & Teachings of Jesus, Life & Letters of Paul, Basic Christian Beliefs,* and *Manners & Customs of Bible Times.*

This particular volume, *New Testament,* provides a quick and easy-to-read overview of the twenty-seven books of the New Testament. You can find a complete listing of all *Shepherd's Notes* on the back cover. It's our prayer that *Shepherd's Notes* will serve you well as you read and live God's Word.

In Him,

David R. Shepherd
Editor-in-Chief

DESIGNED FOR THE BUSY USER

Shepherd's Notes for the New Testament is designed to provide an easy-to-use tool for gaining information on the collection of Bible books the church calls the New Testament. Other *Shepherd's Notes* volumes give a book-by-book presentation of New Testament books. This volume steps back and takes a panoramic view of the New Testament—the books that compose it, the types of literature represented, and the major themes found in these books.

Shepherd's Notes are for laymen, pastors, teachers, small-group leaders and participants, as well as the classroom student. Enrich your personal study or quiet time. Shorten your class or small-group preparation time as you gain valuable insights in the truths of God's Word that you can pass along to your students or group members.

DESIGNED FOR QUICK ACCESS

Those with time restraints will especially appreciate the timesaving features built in the *Shepherd's Notes*. All features are intended to aid a quick and concise encounter with the crux of the message.

Concise Information. The New Testament is replete with characters, places, events, and instruction to believers. Short commentary sections provide quick "snapshots" of sections, highlighting important points and other information.

Brief Outlines. Comprehensive outlines cover each book of the New Testament. This is a valuable feature for following the narrative's flow and allows for a quick, easy way to locate a particular passage.

Shepherd's Notes. These summary statements appear at the beginning of each book's treatment. They deliver the essence of the message presented in the sections that follow.

Icons. Various icons in the margin highlight key insights or themes, allowing the reader to search or trace those themes.

Sidebars and Charts. These specially selected features provide additional background information to aid your study or preparation. These include definitions as well as cultural, historical, and biblical insights.

Maps. These are placed at appropriate places in the book to aid your understanding and study of a text or passage.

In addition to the above features, for those readers who require or desire more information and resources for studying the New Testament, a list of reference sources used for this volume suggests many works that allow readers to extend the scope of their study of the New Testament.

DESIGNED TO WORK FOR YOU

Personal Study. Using the *Shepherd's Notes* with a passage of Scripture can enlighten your study and take it to a new level. At your fingertips is information that would require searching several volumes to find. In addition, many points of application occur throughout the volume, contributing to personal growth.

Teaching Shepherd's Notes: New Testament will be especially valuable for those teaching the Bible. It will enable them to see quickly the larger context of a book or a passage within that book. The outline format, summaries, and sidebars are designed for quick, easy access.

Group Study. *Shepherd's Notes* can be an excellent companion volume to use for gaining a quick but accurate understanding of the message of a Bible book. Each group member can benefit by having his or her own copy. The *Note's* format accommodates the study of each New Testament book. Leaders may use its flexible features to prepare for group sessions or use it during group sessions.

LIST OF MARGIN ICONS USED IN NEW TESTAMENT OVERVIEW

 Shepherd's Notes. Placed to indicate a New Testament book summary. This is a capsule statement that provides the reader with the essence of the message of that particular book.

 Old Testament Passage. An Old Testament prophecy or passage that illuminates the passage being studied.

 New Testament Passage. A New Testament passage that is either a fulfillment of prophecy or is foreshadowed by an Old Testament passage.

 Quote. Used to identify an enlightening quote pertinent to the discussion of the text.

 Word Picture. Indicates that the meaning of a specific word or phrase is illustrated so as to shed light on it.

 Historical Context. To indicate background information—historical, biographical, cultural—and provide insight on understanding or interpreting a passage.

INTRODUCTION TO THE NEW TESTAMENT

The New Testament is the second major division of the Christian Bible with twenty-seven separate works (called "books") attributed to at least eight different writers. This group of writings begins with four accounts of Jesus' life. The first three Gospels (called Synoptics) are similar in content and order. The fourth Gospel differs in order, style, and perspective.

A history of selected events in the early church (Acts of the Apostles) follows the four Gospels and precedes twenty letters to churches and individuals. The last book in the New Testament is an apocalypse—The Revelation. The letters interpret what God did in the life, teachings, death, resurrection, and ascension of Jesus. They also give practical guidance to individual Christians and congregations based on God's revelation in Jesus.

The Revelation is a coded message of hope to the church of the first century which has been reinterpreted by each succeeding generation of Christians for their own situation.

The thirty-nine books of the Old Testament and the twenty-seven books of the New Testament are called the canon. What is a canon? How did just these twenty-seven books become part of it?

THE NEW TESTAMENT CANON

The concept of canon was well understood and accepted by the first Christians. To them, what we now call the Old Testament was Scripture. We do not know the exact process by which the Hebrew Scriptures came to be recognized as

The word *canon* comes from the Greek word for "reed." In the development of the usage of the word, canon came to mean a standard of measurement. Then canon developed to mean an official standard by which other things are measured.

authoritative and qualitatively different than the rest of the Jewish writings.

Although the New Testament documents functioned authoritatively from the beginning, their collection and distinction from other literature of the time was also a gradual process spanning several centuries. We present this process in three stages:

- The First Stage–Oral Transmission and Literary Activity (A.D. 30–90)
- The Second Stage–Collection (A.D. 90–180)
- The Third Stage–An Accepted Canon (A.D. 180–400).

This process naturally arose from the circumstances and outlook of the earliest period of the church. We note four contributing factors:

1. From Jesus Himself the church had learned the importance of the Old Testament. Paul, too, assumed this concept. He spoke of "everything that was written in the past was written to teach us, so that through endurance and the encouragement of the Scriptures we might have hope" (Rom. 15:4). Thus the church had a notion of canon from the very beginning.

2. The notion of canon, as Jesus and the first Christians understood it, was closely connected to the concept of authority. Canonical writings had an authority that other writings didn't have. Authority was inherent in Jesus commissioning the apostles just before His ascension. Irenaeus, in the late second century, considered apostolic witness as the key test of a book being authentic. Even those New Testament writings which were not written by apostles (for example, Mark, Luke, and James) derived their authority

"Don't misunderstand why I have come. I did not come to abolish the law of Moses or the writings of the prophets. No, I came to fulfill them. I assure you, until heaven and earth disappear, even the smallest detail of God's law will remain until its purpose is achieved" (Matt. 5:17–18, NLT).

because of their association with and approval by the apostles.

3. While the New Testament authors made no explicit claims to have been writing Scripture, they did expect at least some of their writings to be circulated among the churches and read in the presence of the congregation (1 Thess. 5:27; Col. 4:16; 1 Cor. 14:37; Rev. 1:3, 11). This practice was similar to the reading of the Old Testament in the synagogue. The letters of Paul were soon placed on a par with the Old Testament—"the other Scriptures" (2 Pet. 3:16).

4. The definition of the canon was also encouraged by the need to preserve the apostolic teaching from distortion by false teachers. Jesus had warned of the coming of false prophets (Matt. 7:15; 24:11, 24; Mark 13:22). His followers reiterated this to their own congregations (2 Cor. 11:13; 2 Pet. 2:1; 1 John 2:26–27; 4:1–6; 2 John 7; Rev. 2:2, 20). The rise of Gnostic teachers in the late first and early second centuries stimulated the church to distinguish authentic writings of the apostles (or "apostolic men" like Luke) from heretical productions.

Among the Apostolic Fathers (about A.D. 96–150) we find no formulated doctrine of Scripture or canon. The common assumption is that the apostolic traditions (whether oral or written) stand alongside the Old Testament as a parallel authority. There are many references to New Testament writings, but only in a few instances are these formally cited as quotations from *Scripture* (Polycarp, *Phil* 12.1; *Barn* 4.14; *2 Clero* 2.4). Ignatius of Antioch (about A.D. 107) may have known a collection of the Pauline Letters.

In the middle of the second century, Marcion of Sinope proposed the first canonical list. His canon rejected the Old Testament in its entirety and accepted ten Pauline Epistles and an edited version of Luke.

The decisive response to Marcion and the Gnostics came from Irenaeus, bishop of Lyons (about A.D. 178–200), in his work *Against All Heresies*. Since there are four principal winds and four points of the compass, he argued, there are four and only four Gospels. Irenaeus is perhaps the first of the Apostolic Fathers to cite the book of Acts explicitly. He definitely cited 1 Peter, 1 and 2 John, Revelation, and all of the Pauline Letters with the exception of Philemon; and there are probably allusions to James and Hebrews. In short, Irenaeus's corpus of authoritative literature closely resembled the shape of the present canon.

The Muratorian Canon probably originated in Rome about A.D. 200. This list represented those books that had been received by the western church as canonical. They were authorized to be read in public worship. This document was named for L.A. Muratori who discovered and published it in the mid 1800s.

A similar picture is given by the Muratorian Canon which recognized the canonicity of all our present twenty-seven books except Hebrews, James, 1 and 2 Peter, and 3 John.

Little further movement occurs in succeeding years. The majority of the books of the New Testament are clearly recognized and accepted. A century or more later, Eusebius of Caesarea (about 260–340) describes the canon under a threefold classification: (1) the recognized books—the four Gospels, Acts, the Pauline Epistles (including Hebrews), 1 Peter, 1 John, and (perhaps) Revelation; (2) the disputed books: those generally accepted—James, Jude, 2 and 3 John—and those that are not genuine—The *Acts* of *Paul*, *The Shepherd of Hermas*, *The Apocalypse of Peter*, *The Epistle of Barnabas*, *The Teachings of the Apostles*, and (perhaps)

Revelation; (3) heretical writings; pseudogospels or acts of some apostle.

In the latter part of the fourth and the beginning of the fifth centuries the majority of the church came to a consensus on the content of the New Testament. The first witness to specify the present twenty-seven books of the New Testament as alone canonical was Athanasias's Easter letter of A.D. 367. At the close of the century the Third Council of Carthage (A.D. 397) prescribed the same list. This was confirmed again at Carthage in A.D. 419.

During the fifth century the present canon became the general consensus of the church. The exceptions are the native (as distinct from the Greek-speaking) Syrian church, which acknowledges only twenty-two books (omitting 2 Peter, 2 and 3 John, Jude, and Revelation). The Ethiopian church accepts the usual twenty-seven but includes another eight books that deal primarily with church order. However, when particular groups of Christians who are in communication with the church at large have studied the question of the extent of the canon, there has been remarkable agreement.

That the canon is closed flows from a confidence that God in His providence not only inspired the authors of Scripture to write exactly those things He wished to communicate to the church but also superintended their preservation and collection.

GENRE IN THE NEW TESTAMENT

The term *genre* is a literary category that denotes the style, form, or general content of a literary production. The question of the genre into which the New Testament writings fit is an important one, and in recent years

"Neither the church councils nor the application of these tests made any book authoritative or authentic. The book was inspired, authoritative, and therefore genuine when it was written. The councils recognized and verified certain books as the written Word of God, and eventually those so recognized were collected in what we call the Bible"—David S. Dockery from *Christian Scripture,* Broadman & Holman Publishers.

discussions about genre have become increasingly prominent.

The issue is significant because understanding the genre of literature provides guidance in reading it correctly.

Four broad categories of genre appear in the New Testament:

- Gospels (Matthew, Mark, Luke, John)
- letters (written by Paul, James, Peter, Jude, and John)
- history (in Acts)
- apocalyptic (in Revelation).

Gospels

The Gospels are similar to biographies but differ from biographies in some respects. The Gospels do not profess to be comprehensive historical accounts of Jesus' life, for they lack details about his childhood and growth into maturity as well as a complete account of His ministry. All four Gospels lack chronological precision in reporting Jesus' life. Each Gospel is written with a specific purpose or aim, and each Gospel writer selected the content of the Gospel with that purpose in mind (note John's guiding purpose in John 20:30–31).

"Jesus' disciples saw him do many other miraculous signs besides the ones recorded in this book. But these are written so that you may believe that Jesus is the Messiah, the Son of God, and that by believing in him you will have life" (John 20:30–31, NLT).

Letters

We may classify Paul's writings as letters, but the defining features of each Pauline letter vary slightly. Romans is a letter that presents a theological argument, and 1 Corinthians is a letter that responds to needs and questions among the Corinthians. A distinctive feature of all of Paul's letters is their occasional nature. Each letter is generally written in response to a specific occasion or need of the church which received it. We will interpret more accurately, the better we understand the situation which produced the letter.

History
The book of Acts contains history, but Luke presents this history with the aid of theological interpretation. The Christian history presented in Acts is not exhaustive, for little report is given of the spread of Christianity in Asia and Africa.

Apocalyptic
The Revelation of John has been called an apocalypse, a prophecy, and an epistle or letter. Traces of all three of these genres appear in Revelation. Apocalyptic characteristics are seen in the extensive use of symbolism, the communication of messages by angels using visions, and an expectation of divine deliverance in the near future (see "near" in Rev. 1:3).

NEW TESTAMENT BACKGROUND—THE INTERTESTAMENTAL PERIOD

The Intertestamental Period concerns the events and writings originating after the final prophet mentioned in the Old Testament (Malachi, about 450 B.C.) and the birth of Christ (about 4 B.C.).

OUTLINE OF INTERTESTAMENTAL PERIOD HISTORY

Shortly after 600 B.C., the Babylonians captured Jerusalem, destroyed the Temple, and took away many of the people as captives. After Cyrus overcame the Babylonian Empire, the Jews who desired were allowed to return. The Temple was rebuilt. Under the leadership of Nehemiah and Ezra, the Jewish religious community established itself, and the worship and life of the people continued. Here Old Testament history ends, and the Intertestamental Period begins. The history of the Intertestamental Period can be divided into three sections:

- The Greek Period, 323 B.C.–167 B.C.
- Period of Independence, 167–63 B.C.
- Roman Period, 63 B.C. through the time of the New Testament.

The influences of the Greek and Roman cultures are prominent in the New Testament. It is within the historical framework provided by the Intertestamental Period that the gospel was born.

LITERATURE OF THE INTERTESTAMENTAL PERIOD

The writings of the Intertestamental Period can be divided into three groups: the Apocrypha,

Pseudepigrapha, and the Qumran Scrolls (Dead Sea Scrolls).

Apocrypha. The Apocrypha are writings that were included, for the most part, in the Greek translation of the Old Testament, the Septuagint. They were translated into Latin and became a part of the Latin Vulgate, the authoritative Latin Bible. Some are historical books. First Maccabees is our chief source for the history of the period from Antiochus Epiphanes to John Hyrcanus. Other books are Wisdom Literature. Others can be classified as historical romances. One is apocalyptic, giving attention to the end of time and God's intervention in history. One writing is devotional in nature.

Pseudepigrapha. A second group of writings is the Pseudepigrapha. It is a larger collection than the Apocrypha, but there is no final agreement as to which writings should be included in it. Fifty-two writings are included in the two volumes, *The Old Testament Pseudepigrapha*, edited by James H. Charlesworth. These cover the range of Jewish thought from apocalyptic to wisdom to devotional. Their titles indicate that they are attributed to noted people of ancient times, such as Adam, Abraham, Enoch, Ezra, and Baruch. For the most part they were written in the last centuries before the birth of Jesus, although some of them are from the first century A.D.

Qumran Scrolls. The final group of writings from this period are the Qumran Scrolls, popularly known as the Dead Sea Scrolls. These writings include Old Testament manuscripts, writings of the Qumran sect, and writings copied and used by the sect which came from other sources. These writings show us something of the life

The first knowledge of the Qumran Scrolls came with the discovery of manuscripts in a cave above the Dead Sea in 1947. During subsequent years, fragments of manuscripts have been found in at least eleven caves in the area.

and beliefs of one group of Jews in the last two centuries before Jesus.

CONCLUSION

An understanding of the Intertestamental Period is critical to the study of the Bible, for New Testament times and thinking were greatly influenced by the events of this period and the philosophies that emerged and developed during this four-hundred-year span of time.

ORDER OF THE GOSPELS

The question of relationship between our Gospels is often discussed, but not easily answered. This is especially so when attention is focused on the Gospels of Matthew, Mark, and Luke, the popularly designated "Synoptic Gospels."

The term *Synoptic* means *to see together* or *to view from a common perspective*. The first three Gospels are so identified because they present the life and ministry of Jesus from a common point of view that is different from that of the Gospel of John.

In general the Synoptics follow the same outline and record similar material. Sometimes their accounts are almost identical. Yet at other times important differences are observed. This phenomena has given rise, especially in the modern era, to what is called "the Synoptic problem."

How are we to understand and explain the literary relationship of these three Gospels? John's Gospel is usually dated later than the Synoptics (A.D. 80–95), and no extensive literary dependence is readily discerned. Therefore we will note the more popular theories as they pertain to the Synoptic Gospels.

Primitive Gospel Theory

This position suggests that our three biblical or canonical Gospels drew their material from an earlier, more primitive gospel that has not been preserved, probably written in Aramaic. This view has little if any historical support.

Oral Tradition Theory

This view believes that only an "oral gospel" is behind our Synoptic Gospels. This theory emphasizes that the Gospel material was passed along orally or by word of mouth before being written down. There is some truth in this theory, but it is insufficient to account for (a) the possible existence of early written accounts (see Luke 1:1-3), (b) the different order of events discovered in the Synoptics, and (c) the variations in form, content, vocabulary, grammar, and word order that are evident in our Synoptic Gospels.

MARKAN PRIORITY

This theory is the most popular theory among contemporary Bible students. It was not advocated until the modern era and the rise of historical criticism. This theory initially began as a two-source theory but is now usually expanded into a four-source theory.

Mark is viewed as the first Gospel written and is the foundation of Matthew and Luke, who incorporated almost all of Mark. Matthew and Luke also utilized another source (usually assumed to have been written) commonly called Q, from the German word *Quelle*, meaning *source*. This second source is said to account for about 250 verses of mostly teaching material of Jesus common to Matthew and Luke but that is not in Mark.

Expanding the two-source theory, an M-source is thought to account for material unique to Matthew, and an L-source is hypothetically set forth to account for material peculiar to Luke. Though the most popular theory, this model faces the difficulties of (a) having no early church support and (b) claiming sources (Q, L, M) with no historical support for their existence.

Matthean Priority

Matthean priority was the position of the church from the first century until the Enlightenment. This theory sees Matthew as the first Synoptic, Luke, who utilized Matthew, as second, and Mark as third, being an abbreviated combination of Matthew and Luke.

The preaching of Peter is also seen as a significant influence on Mark's Gospel. The strengths of this theory are that (a) it was the unanimous view of the early church, and (b) it can account for the literary relationship that exists between the Synoptic Gospels without assuming hypothetical documents with little or no historical support.

While we do not know for sure how the Gospel writers possibly interacted with one another or what sources may have influenced their work, we are confident that the result of their work has given us three inspired, truthful, and authoritative portraits of our Lord Jesus Christ.

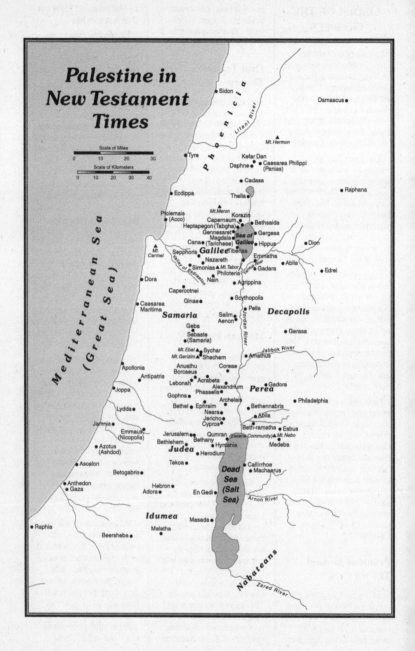

Palestine in
New Testament
Times

Scale of Miles
0   10   20   30

Scale of Kilometers
0   10   20   30   40

Phoenicia

Litani River

Sidon

Damascus

Mt. Hermon

Tyre

Kefar Dan
Daphne   Caesarea Philippi
            (Panias)

Cadasa

Ecdippa

Thella

Raphana

Ptolemais
(Acco)

Mt. Meron

Korazin
Capernaum   Bethsaida
Heptapegon (Tabgha)
Gennesaret   Sea of   Gergesa
Magdala   Galilee
Cana   (Tarichae)   Hippus   Dion
Sepphoris   Tiberias

Mt.
Carmel

Galilee
Nazareth   Emmatha
Simonias Mt. Tabor   Abila
            Philoteria   Gadara
Nain   Agrippina   Edrei

Valley of Esdraelon

Dora

Capercotnei

Scythopolis

Ginae

Mediterranean Sea

(Great Sea)

Caesarea
Maritima

Samaria

Salim
Aenon

Decapolis

Geba
Sebaste
(Samaria)

Pella

Gerasa

Jordan River

Mt. Ebal   Sychar
Mt. Gerizim   Shechem

Anuathu
Borcaeus

Coreae

Amathus

Jabbok River

Apollonia

Antipatris

Lebonah   Acrabeta
        Alexandrium
Phasaelis

Gadora

Perea

Philadelphia

Joppa

Gophna
        Archelais
Bethel   Ephraim   Neara
        Jericho
        Cyprus

Bethennabris
Abila

Lydda

Jamnia
Emmaus
(Nicopolis)
Azotus
(Ashdod)

Jerusalem   Qumran (Essene Community)   Esbus
Bethlehem   Bethany   Mt. Nebo
        Hyrcania   Medeba
Judea   Herodium

Beth-ramatha

Ascalon

Tekoa

Dead
Sea
(Salt
Sea)

Callirrhoe
Machaerus

Betogabris

Anthedon
Gaza

Hebron
Adora

En Gedi

Arnon River

Idumea   Masada

Raphia

Malatha

Beersheba

Nabateans

Zered River

MATTHEW

OVERVIEW

■ *Matthew in a Nutshell. This first Gospel*
■ *affirms that Jesus is the King, the Messiah,*
■ *who has come and whose reign has begun.*
■ *Several Old Testament texts included in Mat-*
■ *thew support the claim that Jesus is the ful-*
■ *fillment of messianic expectations. Also, the*
■ *Gospel ends with the affirmation that all*
■ *authority in heaven and on earth has been*
■ *given to Christ (28:18), which means that*
■ *His reign continues.*

Matthew's Gospel is easily divided into seven sections: a beginning and an end with five teaching sections between. The beginning section is the account of Jesus' birth. The last section is the narrative of Jesus crucifixion and resurrection.

Each of the five middle sections of Matthew is built around a major discourse of Jesus. The five discourse sections are:

- the Sermon on the Mount (Matt. 5–7)
- the instruction to the Twelve for their mission (Matt. 10)
- the parables of the kingdom (Matt. 13)
- the teaching about the church (Matt. 18)
- the teaching concerning things to come (Matt. 24).

The narrative of Jesus' actions that precedes or follows these major discourses are linked to these discourses.

Background. Early church tradition unanimously ascribes this Gospel to Matthew—also known as Levi, one of Jesus' twelve apostles, and a converted tax collector (9:9–13; 10:31). Although modern scholarship has called this identification into repeated question, there are no persuasive reasons for rejecting this tradition outright.

"Matthew demonstrates that Jesus and his church were the fulfillment of all God's promises to Israel"—Craig L. Blomberg, *Matthew*, New American Commentary (Nashville: Broadman & Holman Publishers, 1992), 21.

Two early church fathers, Irenaeus and Origen wrote that Matthew wrote for a Jewish audience. This is born out of Matthew's extensive quoting from the Old Testament. A.T. Robertson's *Word Pictures in the New Testament* lists ninety-three quotations in Matthew, forty-nine in Mark, eighty in Luke, and thirty-three in John.

Matthew 1–4. This first section opens the Gospel with the royal genealogy and builds to the proclamation of God in 3:17: "This is my Son, whom I love." The genealogies confirm Jesus' authoritative, kingly lineage and remind the reader of His relation to all nations by mentioning Tamar, Rahab, Ruth, and Solomon's mother, Bathsheba, the wife of a Hittite. When Jesus came to John for baptism, the voice from heaven proclaimed Him as God's Son. As God's Son, Jesus had the authority and power to confront Satan and overcome. Jesus then went to Galilee of the Gentiles (4:15) to begin His public ministry. This opening section makes it obvious that Jesus is designated by God to be the Messiah with authority—for all nations.

Matthew 5–7. The Sermon on the Mount is one of the best known passages in the New Testament. Here Jesus announces that He has not come to do away with the Law but to bring it to completion—to fulfill it. Here Jesus says that not only is behavior important but the attitudes and motives from which behavior flow are of great importance. For that reason, Jesus' standards are even more exacting than the Law as traditionally understood.

Matthew 8–10. This passage opens with a series of ten miracles demonstrating Jesus' authority over disease, natural catastrophes, demons, and death. His hearers were amazed at Jesus' teachings on the Mount. Now amazement is the reaction to Jesus' powerful deeds. His disciples wondered that "even the winds and waves obey him!" (8:27), and the crowds stood amazed that He had the authority to forgive sins (9:8). By continuing the emphasis on authority, teaching, and Gentiles, Jesus prepared His immediate disciples for their task after His death.

Matthew 11:1–13:52. People had a variety of reactions to Jesus' deeds. When the leaders reject Jesus' authority in chapter 12, Matthew implies that Jesus will go to the Gentiles by quoting Isaiah the prophet (12:18–21). Jesus continues His teaching in parables to those who are willing to listen (13:10–13).

Matthew 13:53–18:35. Jesus teaches in the synagogue in His hometown, Nazareth. The people have the same response to Jesus' teaching as the crowds did at the end of the Sermon on the Mount. They are astonished (compare 13:54; 7:28). Although Jesus presents His authoritative teaching, His hometown people reject it (13:57). His disciples accept Him (14:33), and so does the Gentile woman (15:22). Jesus takes His disciples aside and asks them who He is. Peter confesses that Jesus is the Messiah. (16:16). Jesus goes on to explain to His disciples what kind of Messiah He is so as to prepare them for what will soon take place.

Matthew 19–25. Jesus' ministry in Galilee comes to an end. He begins the last journey to Jerusalem. Jesus dramatically presents His kingly authority by His triumphal entry into Jerusalem (21:1–9) and by cleansing the Temple (21:10–17). Then, while He is teaching, the chief priests and elders challenge Him saying, "By what authority are you doing these things?" (21:23). Jesus answers with parables and other teachings (21:28–22:46). Jesus warns the people about the examples of the Pharisees and Sadducees (23:1–38). He then concentrates His teaching only on His disciples (24:1–25:46).

Matthew 26–28. While Jesus was in Jerusalem, the religious leaders find their opportunity to try Him and have the Romans put him to death. In

Jesus is the Messiah prophesied by Scripture. Matthew emphasized the fact that Jesus was the Jews expected Messiah. The term *messiah* means "Anointed One." It had come to signify the ideal king, David's descendant, who would free the Jews from Roman rule and establish an earthly kingdom. Jesus did not accept this understanding of messiahship. He was the messianic King, but He chose to take on the role of Isaiah's Suffering Servant (Isa. 52:13–53:12). By His death He provides freedom from sin, not from foreign rule.

the midst of the trial scene Jesus is asked if He is the Messiah. Jesus responds by affirming His authority: "Yes, it is as you say" (26:64). Pilate, a Gentile, recognizes Jesus' kingly authority, placarding over the cross: "THIS IS JESUS, THE KING OF THE JEWS" (27:37).

Jesus died within six hours of being crucified. His body was claimed by a wealthy Jewish leader, Joseph of Arimathea, who gave Jesus' body a dignified burial in a tomb he had bought for himself. The third day Jesus was raised from death. Over a period of weeks He met with His disciples, preparing them for a time when He would not be physically present with them. Matthew's Gospel closes with Jesus' commission to His disciples (28:18–20).

Of the four Gospel writers only Matthew includes teachings about the church. He deals with the basis of this new community of faith (16:17–19) and provides other teachings relating to the church (18:15–20). He stressed Jesus' call of His church to preach His gospel to all the world and to nurture believers into full maturity (28:16–20).

MARK

OVERVIEW

- *Mark in a Nutshell. Mark opens with "The*
- *beginning of the gospel about Jesus Christ,*
- *the Son of God" (1:1). Near the end of*
- *Mark's account, at the death of Jesus, a*
- *Roman centurion says of Jesus, "Surely this*
- *man was the Son of God!"(15:39). From*
- *beginning to end, Mark presented Jesus the*
- *Messiah as the strong Son of God.*

The Gospel of Mark is a fast-paced narrative—an action-packed account of Jesus' ministry which focuses on Jesus as a servant who exercises power to free human beings from disease, demons, death, and danger. Unlike Matthew and Luke, Mark doesn't give an account of Jesus' birth. Neither does Mark give the detailed account of Jesus' teachings that are found in Matthew, Luke, and John.

Mark 1–9. Mark begins with the public ministry of John, the baptism of Jesus, and only briefly mentions the initial temptations of Jesus (1:1–13). Again, as in Matthew, the ministry in Galilee (1:14–9:50) occupies a great portion of Mark's Gospel. The Galilean ministry can be divided into three periods.

The first begins with the arrest of John the Baptist (1:14). The second comes with Jesus's call of the Twelve Disciples (3:13–19). The third coincides with a growing hostility toward Jesus on the part of the religious leaders. Jesus then retires to the region of Tyre and Sidon and

Background.
According to church tradition, John Mark wrote the second Gospel from Rome, using Peter as his primary source. John Mark's mother hosted a Jerusalem house church (Acts 12:12), and he ministered alongside his cousin Barnabas (Acts 12:25; 15:37, 39), Paul (Col. 4:10; 2 Tim. 4:11; Phil. 24), and later Peter (1 Pet. 5:13).
Jewish-Christians were likely in Rome in A.D.45 when Claudius expelled the Jews over the "Christos" disturbance (see Acts 18:2). Mark shows signs that it was written to a largely Gentile church; for example, explaining Aramaic expressions (5:41; 7:34; 14:36; 15:34) and the Pharisees' traditions (7:3–4).

"For even the Son of Man did not come to be served, but to serve, and to give his life as a ransom for many" (Mark 10:45).

focuses His efforts on the training of the Twelve (7:24–30).

The turning point in Mark occurs during this time of withdrawal. Jesus takes His disciples into the region of Caesarea Philippi. There He asks them who He is. Peter confesses that Jesus is the Messiah. Jesus then begins to explain the difference between who He is and the then current expectations of Messiah. In this context Jesus emphasizes that to be a disciple of the Messiah is to take the same path of suffering and cross-bearing (8:27–9:1).

"If anyone would come after me, he must deny himself and take up his cross and follow me" (Matt. 8:34).

Mark 10–16. The first verse of chapter 10 marks the beginning of new stage in Jesus' ministry. Chapter 10 quickly shows a transition from Galilee to Judea, preparing his readers for Passion Week (chaps. 11–15) and the resurrection (chap. 16). Mark leaves out many details in Jesus' transition from Galilee to Jerusalem. Almost forty percent of Mark's Gospel is focused on Passion Week and Jesus' resurrection.

Mark portrays Jesus as a man possessing every human emotion. Moved by compassion, anger, frustration, mercy, and sorrow (1:41; 3:5; 8:17; 14:6,33), Jesus ministered among His own kind. Mark offers the full humanity of Jesus without reservation (see 3:21; 4:38; 6:3–6; 13:32); from the beginning of His earthly ministry (2:20), Jesus lived in the ominous shadow of the cross until the agony of Gethsemane almost overwhelmed Him (14:34). While Jesus is man, He is also the strong Son of God who suffers and dies. He is victorious in His living, His dying, and, most importantly, in His resurrection.

Mark's Gospel was designed to evoke faith in the deity of Jesus: the divine voice announced it from heaven, demons screamed it in agony, Peter professed it boldly, even a Roman centurion acknowledged it (15:39). Mark's readers knew struggle and suffering; and in learning from and following their Master, they could be victorious, too.

Background. Luke's Gospel, according to church tradition, was written by the sometime companion of Paul, Luke. This is indicated by the "we" passages in Acts 16:10–17; 20:5–15; 21:1–18; 27:1–28:16. He likely was a medical doctor, possibly from Antioch of Syria. Though he was not Jewish, it is not known whether he was a native Syrian or a Greek. No one knows the locale from which Luke wrote his Gospel.

"Today in the town of David a Savior has been born to you; he is Christ the Lord" (Luke 2:11).

OVERVIEW

- *Luke in a Nutshell. Luke is the most complete*
- *single account available of the life of Jesus.*
- *What we have is a portrait of Jesus as Savior.*
- *He is Savior to His own people and to all peo-*
- *ples. This theme is announced at the outset*
- *and is presented in many variations through-*
- *out this Gospel. It is seen in the way Jesus*
- *relates to people as well as in the parables*
- *that are unique to Luke's Gospel.*

Luke has a number of similarities in structure with both Matthew and Mark. All three Gospels show initial ministry, rising opposition, preparation of the Twelve, and final journey to Jerusalem.

Luke 1–2. Luke and Matthew begin their accounts even before Jesus' birth. Luke 1–2 has material that only Mary, Jesus' mother, could have known. Luke shows the family relationship between John the Baptist and Jesus. Even from the outset, Luke presents Jesus as Son of God (1:35) but also as a human being who is born, circumcised as a son of the covenant (2:21), and who goes through the developmental stages that all children go through. Luke is the only Gospel that gives us a glimpse of Jesus as a child (2:41–52).

Luke 3–4:13. Luke shows Jesus' relationship with John the Baptist in their young adult years. Here we are introduced to John's vocation,

Jesus' baptism, His genealogy, and His initial temptations.

Luke 4:14–9:50. This account of Jesus' Galilean ministry begins at the synagogue in Jesus' hometown of Nazareth, an event that only Luke reported. Even at the outset, Jesus stirred hostility when He reminded His listeners of God's grace to Gentiles at several points in Israel's history. Luke's presentation of Jesus' ministry in Galilee has parallels in either Matthew or Mark or both. In the events that only Luke narrates, we see emphases that are important to Luke. Women receive significant attention in Luke's Gospel. Luke told of a sinful woman's anointing Jesus' feet in the home of a Pharisee named Simon (7:36–50). Only Luke wrote that when Jesus began His second tour of Galilee several women joined Him and the Twelve. These women provided economic support to Jesus' ministry.

Luke 9:51–19:27. Jesus left Galilee and went to minister in Judea and Perea by way of Samaria. Much of the material in this section is unique to Luke. Here we have one of the best-known stories in the Bible, the parable of the Good Samaritan (10:25–37). Prayer is of special interest to Luke. In this section are three parables about prayer (11:1–13; 18:1–14). Here also is a chapter that underscores Luke's theme of Jesus as Savior. Chapter 15 contains the parables of the lost sheep, the lost coin, and the lost son. These parables have the same effect on religious leaders in Judea as Jesus' inaugural message in the synagogue in Nazareth had at the outset of His public ministry.

Luke 19:28–24:53. Jesus' final journey to Jerusalem, His last week, His trial and Crucifixion

"Then he went down to Nazareth with them and was obedient to them. But his mother treasured all these things in her heart. And Jesus grew in wisdom and stature, and in favor with God and men" (Luke 2:51–52).

Jesus' last encounter in this section is with Zacchaeus, the despised tax collector. A life-changing transformation came as a result. Jesus commented on this event with what might well be the overall theme of Luke's Gospel: "For the Son of Man came to seek and to save what was lost" (19:10).

Two of Jesus' seven words on the cross are found only in Luke.

"Father, forgive them, for they do not know what they are doing" (Luke 23:34).

"Father, into your hands I commit my spirit" (Luke 23:46).

"The encouraging phrase 'Do not be afraid' is found often in Luke's Gospel, for the message of salvation replaces fear with joy. All kinds of people heard it: Zacharias (1:13), Mary (1:30), the shepherds (2:10), Peter 5:10, Jairus (8:50), and the disciples (12:7, 32)"—Warren W. Wiersbe, *With the Word* (Nashville: Oliver Nelson, 1991), 669.

have parallels in at least one and sometimes more than one other Gospel. As Jesus' bore His cross to Golgotha, a passage unique to Luke tells about women along the Via Dolorosa crying and lamenting Him (23:27). Only Luke's Gospel tells of Jesus' forgiving those who crucified Him. Luke was the only Gospel writer to write about the exchange between Jesus and the two thieves who were crucified alongside Jesus. Here we see Jesus' power to save in the most extreme situations for Him and for the thief, as He promised: "I tell you the truth, today you will be with me in paradise" (23:43).

Mark's Gospel gives only a glimpse of Jesus' Resurrection appearance to the two disciples on the road to Emmaus. Luke researched this event in great detail and provided an unforgettable account of the risen Christ joining Cleopas and his companion. These disciples were downcast over the events that had transpired. Shock and grief kept them from recognizing the One for whom they grieved. As they walked, He gave them a survey of the Hebrew Scriptures, pointing out in each section of Scripture what they should have anticipated about Messiah. When they arrived at their destination, they invited Jesus to join them for a meal. As they broke bread and gave thanks, they recognized Him.

JOHN

OVERVIEW

■ *John in a Nutshell. The theme of John's Gos-*
■ *pel is the Incarnation—God in human form*
■ *in the person of Jesus Christ. For this reason,*
■ *John's Gospel is often seen as the most evan-*
■ *gelistic of the four Gospels. John's emphasis*
■ *is on the nature of Christ as opposed to the*
■ *more chronological, historical accounts of*
■ *Jesus' life in Matthew, Mark, and Luke. John*
■ *clearly stated his purpose: "But these are*
■ *written that you may believe that Jesus is the*
■ *Christ, the Son of God, and that by believing*
■ *you may have life in his name" (20:31).*

John's Gospel has many differences in compari-
son with the Synoptics. Below are some of the
similarities and differences.

John	*Synoptics*
Similarities	
John the Baptist as forerunner of Jesus	
The call of some of the disciples	
Jesus as One who both taught and wrought miracles	
The growing opposition to Jesus from the religious leaders	
Jesus' Passion and Resurrection	
Differences	
Jesus' person	
Jesus' relationship to the Father	Kingdom of God

Background. The authorship of John's Gospel has been traditionally ascribed to the Apostle John, the son of Zebedee and the brother of James. The Gospel exhibits many marks that suggest it was written by one who was an eyewitness to the life and ministry of Jesus, such as the aroma of the broken perfume jar in the house at Bethany (12:3). Polycarp (c. A.D. 70–155), bishop of Smyrna, was a disciple of John. Polycarp's disciple, Irenaeus, affirmed that John wrote the Gospel that bears his name. Both Clement of Alexandria and Origen hold to John the Apostle as author.

It is possible to translate "may believe" in John's purpose statement as "may continue to believe," which would intimate the purpose not only of winning individuals to faith in Christ but also of strengthening the family of faith already walking with Christ.

23

John	*Synoptics*
Focus on Judean ministry	Focus on Galilean ministry
Three Passovers	One Passover
Jesus' preexistence	Jesus' birth and childhood

John's presentation of Jesus as the One through whom life comes is evident in the structure of the book.

John 1. John went beyond time to show that Jesus is identical with the Word—the Second Person of the Trinity. The Word (*Logos*) has always existed and was the agent through whom the worlds were created. John said it so simply. The Word became a human being at a particular place and time. This introduction tells us when and where the Word became a human being; introduces His forerunner, John the Baptist; and foretells the opposition Jesus will encounter.

Included in this section is perhaps the best-known verse in the Bible: "For God so loved the world that he gave his one and only Son, that whoever believes in him shall not perish but have eternal life" (3:16).

John 2–11. This section has sometimes been called the Book of Signs. John selected seven of the many miracles Jesus performed to convey His person and purpose. The signs are:

1. Changing water to wine at a wedding (2:1–11)
2. Healing the royal official's son at Capernaum (4:46–54)
3. Healing the paralyzed man at the pool of Bethesda (5:1–15)
4. Feeding the five thousand (6:1–15)
5. Walking on the Sea of Tiberias (6:16–24)
6. Healing a blind man (9:1–34)
7. Raising Lazarus from the dead (11:1–44).

The signs were a double-edged sword. To some, they inspired faith. To others, they brought increased hostility and resistance. John's comments following the first and seventh sign illustrate this.

John 12–20. This section of John is called the Book of the Passion. Following the raising of Lazarus, the opposition developed a strategy and began its implementation. John included a significant amount of unique material in these chapters. Here is the only account of Jesus' washing His disciples' feet (13:1–17). The next passage details Jesus' intensive preparation of the disciples for the time when He would no longer be physically present. He promised that He would ask the Father and the Father would send "another Counselor" to abide with them forever (14:15).

The Gospel of John brings unique insights to Jesus' trial and Crucifixion. Only in John do we see Jesus' entrusting the care of Mary, His mother, to John. Both this and John's other two words from the cross are unique. (John 19:28, 30).

John 21. The final section of this Gospel presents several Resurrection appearances of Jesus that aren't presented in the other three Gospels. Also, John included Jesus' reinstatement of Peter, who denied Jesus after His arrest (21:15–17). John ended with a statement of the impossibility of really presenting all the glory of Jesus in one book (21:25).

"Therefore many of the Jews who had come to visit Mary, and had seen what Jesus did, put their faith in him. But some of them wen to the Pharisees and told them what Jesus had done. Then the chief priests and the Pharisees called a meeting of the Sanhedrin. . . . So from that day on they plotted to take his life" (John 11:45–47, 53).

Greek has two words for *another*. In this case, the Greek word means another one of the same kind. The Holy Spirit is just like Jesus (14:15).

OVERVIEW

- *Acts in a Nutshell. The major theme of the*
- *book of Acts is the universal, unhindered*
- *spread of the gospel. Aided by the ministry of*
- *the Holy Spirit, the good news spread from a*
- *small group of followers in Jerusalem to*
- *encompass the "ends of the earth" (Acts 1:8).*

Acts was designed to complete a two-volume work and is the companion volume to the Gospel of Luke. In fact, for much of its early history, the two volumes circulated together. When the early church decided on the form of the New Testament we now have, Acts was separated from Luke by John. This was due to the desire to begin the New Testament with the four Gospels.

Acts shows the universal, unhindered spread of the gospel. With the constant aid of the Holy Spirit, the gospel grew from a small group of followers in Jerusalem to encompass the "ends of the earth" (Acts 1:8). Jesus' commission suggests a picture of concentric circles: Jerusalem, Judea, Samaria, the ends of the earth. Acts shows Jesus in His church—breaking through barriers of race, religion, culture, and nationality; moving from place to place to include all people who believe under God's kingly rule in Jesus Christ. Luke highlighted this theme throughout the book. The last word in the Greek text is "unhindered," as Luke described Paul's preaching in Rome. The gospel is triumphant in Acts; nothing could stop its spread.

Background. Traditionally, Luke has been seen as the author of both the Gospel and Acts. We know little about Luke. He is referred to as a doctor in Colossians and a dear friend to Paul. From other places in the New Testament, one can conclude that Luke was a Gentile. Some have suggested that Luke came from Macedonia and was part of Paul's vision to preach the gospel in Greece (Acts 16). Others have suggested that Luke was a native of Antioch in Syria.

"But you will receive power when the Holy Spirit comes on you; and you will be my witnesses in Jerusalem, and in all Judea and Samaria, and to the ends of the earth" (1:8).

This major theme has two subthemes:

1. The acceptance of the gospel by Gentiles and the incorporation of Gentiles into the church which was almost completely Jewish.
2. The rejection of the gospel by official Judaism.

Even though the beginning of Acts portrays the church as continuing to worship in the Temple and in the synagogue, Acts chronicles an increasing separation between the two groups.

Luke's statement in the first two verses of Acts contrasts the purpose of the third Gospel, Luke, with the purpose of Acts. The Gospel of Luke was an account of what Jesus began to do and to teach up to the Ascension. Acts is an account of the continuation of Jesus' work through the Holy Spirit at work in the early church.

Acts 1–5. Luke began this second volume of his work with a prologue that parallels the prologue in his Gospel. He then presented Jesus' commission to His disciples and His Ascension. Part of His command to them was to wait in Jerusalem for the promised gift—the Holy Spirit.

The Spirit came days later during the Jewish festival of Pentecost when the faithful from all around the Mediterranean basin were in Jerusalem. The manifestations of the Spirit's presence were so tangible that Peter had the opportunity to explain to the crowd at the Temple what these things meant.

In response to Peter's preaching, three thousand became believers in Jesus as Messiah. Many of these were from Jerusalem and constituted the church in Jerusalem.

Acts 6–12. A wave of persecution followed the martyrdom of Stephen. The result was that the believers carried the gospel beyond Jerusalem into Judea and Samaria. Peter and Philip are prominent in this part of Luke's account.

The first of three accounts of Saul of Tarsus' conversion takes place in this section. The fact that Luke included three accounts of this event indicates the weight and significance he gave to it.

Acts 13:1–21:16. Paul, formerly Saul of Tarsus, became the primary character in this section of Acts. Although his first priority in every city was to present the gospel in the local synagogue, he became the apostle who understood the implications of the Gospel for Gentiles, communicated the gospel to various Gentile cultures, and made it possible for them to be incorporated into the church without becoming Jews.

Acts 21:17–28:31. Paul's missionary activities aroused strong opposition from official Judaism. The result was that he was arrested in Jerusalem. If not for the Romans, he would have been put to death immediately. This section of Acts details his imprisonment by the Romans, his three judicial procedures, and his journey to Rome where he would appeal to Caesar. Acts closes with Paul being under house arrest in Rome. Luke said he had considerable freedom to proclaim the gospel in those circumstances. Acts does not tell the outcome of Paul's appeal to Caesar.

"But the Lord said to Ananias, 'Go! This man [Saul] is my chosen instrument to carry my name before the Gentiles and their kings and before the people of Israel. I will show him how much he must suffer for my name'" (Acts 9:15).

The book of Acts reminds us that our purpose as God's people is to be on mission for Him.

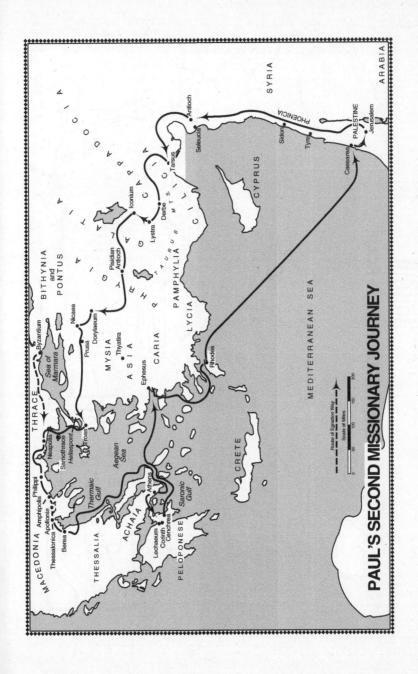

PAUL'S SECOND MISSIONARY JOURNEY

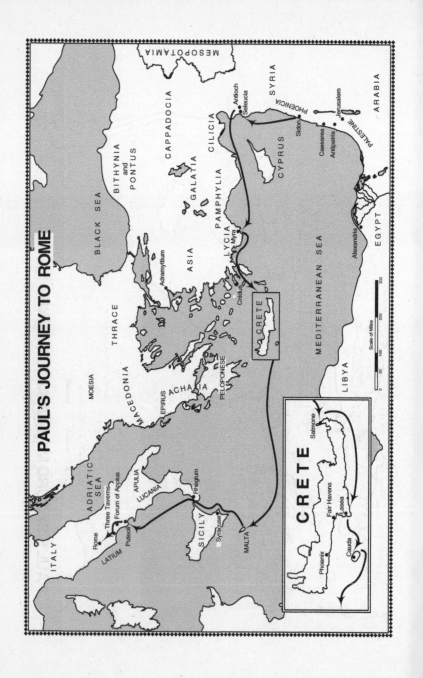

PAUL'S JOURNEY TO ROME

ROMANS

OVERVIEW

■ *Romans in a Nutshell. The theme of the letter*
■ *is the gospel—"the power of God for the sal-*
■ *vation of everyone who believes" (1:16–17).*
■ *Paul articulated the gospel and its practical*
■ *implications for the church at Rome.*

Paul understood the importance and influence of having a strong church in Rome. He wanted to strengthen the existing work in that place initially through the letter and secondly by visiting them (1:8–15; 15:14–33). For this reason Paul methodically and systematically outlined the foundational meaning of salvation in Jesus Christ, the foundation of Christianity. He described the human condition, the meaning of the gospel, God's plan for men and women, God's purpose for Israel, and the responsibilities of the Christian life and ministry.

Romans 1:1–17. Paul's introduction to the letter (vv. 1–15) sets out the apostolic calling which qualifies him (vv. 1–7) and explains his reason for writing this letter (vv. 8–15). After the introduction, Paul crisply stated the theme of his letter—the righteousness of God, revealed in the gospel and bringing salvation (vv. 16–17).

Romans 1:18–3:20. Paul then supported his theme in the first major section of the letter by demonstrating that all persons need salvation, showing first that the power of sin rules the Gentiles (1:18–32) and, second, that the power of sin rules the Jews as well (2:1–3:8). Paul

Background. Romans has been called the most important letter ever written. Paul wrote his letter to the Romans from Corinth during his third missionary journey around A.D. 56–57 (Acts 20:2–3).

"Therefore no one will be declared righteous in his [God's] sight by observing the law; rather, through the law we become conscious of sin" (Rom. 3:20).

concluded this section with a summary statement that all humanity stands under the power of sin (3:19–20).

Romans 3:21–4:25. The second major section deals with God's provision of righteousness through Jesus Christ on the basis of faith. The question Paul dealt with is how a holy, righteous God continues to be just and to justify persons who have violated His law and have the ongoing tendency to do so. The answer is that God has taken the punishment for sin in His Son, Jesus. Those who have faith in Jesus' blood stand in right relationship with God. Justification by faith is not achieved through strict obedience to the Law. The way God justified Abraham by faith demonstrates that trust as a way of relating to God preceded seeking to relate to Him by the works of the Law, meeting the Jewish objection that God requires works for justification (3:27–4:25).

Romans 5–8. After establishing the reality of justification by faith, Paul discussed, in the third section of Romans, the impact and implication of what God does for us in Christ and focuses on how salvation results in a victorious new life. The immediate result of justification is a realization of peace with God based on the assurance coming from God's love for us and results in our ability to rejoice in the face of difficulties because Christ has reversed the results of Adam's disobedience (5:1–21). The very heart of salvation is found in the Christian's continuing, but victorious, struggle with sin (6:1–7:25). This victorious struggle is possible because of the power of the risen Christ, experienced as Holy Spirit, who helps us to do what is right (8:1–39).

"We have been made right with God because of our faith. Now we have peace with him because of our Lord Jesus Christ." (Rom. 5:1, NIRV).

Romans 9–11. The salvation Christ brought raised profound questions among Jewish Christians about the destiny of the Jews who still felt themselves to be God's people even though they had rejected Christ. Paul dealt with this issue in the fourth section. He stressed that the righteousness of God is demonstrated in His faithfulness to all His promises—even those to Israel in the Old Testament. Paul confessed his personal grief over Israel's rejection of Christ (9:1–15) and affirmed that God has, as always, displayed His sovereignty in dealing with Israel (9:6–29). Israel's God-given freedom to choose explains the rejection of Jesus as the Christ (9:30–10:21). Paul reminded his readers that Israel's rejection of the Messiah is not permanent. God's love of and election of Israel is irrevocable. Both Jews and Gentiles will receive mercy (11:1–36).

Romans 12:1–15:13. The final section of Romans is a summons to practical obedience to God. Christians should live transformed lives (12:1–2) and demonstrate this in a good stewardship of their spiritual gifts (12:3–21), in fulfilling their obligations to the state (13:1–7), in making love supreme (13:8–14), and in seeking to nurture others in the fellowship of the church, being particularly careful to bear with and edify the weak (14:1–15:13).

CONCLUSION

Romans 15:14–16:27. In the conclusion to the letter, Paul summarized his ministry and his plans for the future, requesting their prayers (15:14–33); then he commended Phoebe (16:1–2), sent greetings to individual Christians (16:3–24), and ended his letter with praise for God (16:27).

OVERVIEW

Background. The letter (1:1–2; 16:21) as well as church tradition acknowledge Paul as the author of 1 Corinthians. This affirmation generally has gone unchallenged. The letter was written around A.D. 55 near the end of Paul's three-year ministry in Ephesus (1 Cor. 16:5–9; Acts 20:31).

■ *1 Corinthians in a Nutshell. First Corin-*
■ *thians deals with a number of problems that*
■ *have arisen in a church planted in a notori-*
■ *ously pagan culture.*

Paul went to Corinth on his second missionary journey and began teaching immediately in the synagogue there. While some of the Jews believed, leaders and others of the synagogue rejected his witness. He continued his work through the home of Titius Justus, a Gentile who lived next door to the synagogue (Acts 18:7). Although Paul met resistance, the work went well, and a struggling church began with even Crispus, the synagogue ruler and his family becoming Christians (Acts 18:7–8).

1 Corinthians 1:1–9. Paul expressed thanks for the spiritual gifts God had given to the Corinthians and for their exercising of those gifts.

1 Corinthians 1:10–3:4. Reports of divisions within the church had come to Paul from Chloe's family, and Paul addresses those divisions. The Corinthians were impressed by those who claimed to be wise. Paul contrasted the foolishness of God with the wisdom of man (1:25).

1 Corinthians 3:5–4:21. Human leaders play important roles in the church, but all of them are servants. Christ Jesus is the unchanging foundation of the church.

1 Corinthians 5–6. The sexual immorality on the part of one of the Corinthians is not something to boast about but a matter of profound grief and sorrow. The church should be proactive in dealing with this brother with a view to bringing him to repentance.

1 Corinthians 7. God has ordained marriage and has set forth guidelines that make it a blessing. Paul's counsel is that not everyone should get married. Those who are married to an unbeliever should continue in that marriage.

1 Corinthians 8:1–11:1. Christians should think carefully about eating meat which has been offered to idols and then is sold in the marketplace. There is nothing intrinsically wrong with the meat, but many new Christians are offended when they see others participating in a practice that they see as contrary to their new life in Christ.

1 Corinthians 11:2–34. The Corinthians needed to give attention to their attitude and behavior in public worship, especially the Lord's Supper.

When considering an action, we have more than our own conscience to consider. We should consider the effect our action will have on the consciences of other believers.

1 Corinthians 12–14. Spiritual gifts are imparted not to boost egos but for the good of the entire body of Christ. In this context, Paul said that the Corinthians should desire the greater gifts. Love should guide the exercising of spiritual gifts. Paul gave a beautifully detailed description of love.

1 Corinthians 15. Paul reminded the Corinthians of the basics of the gospel. Jesus' Resurrection—well attested as a historical fact—is one of those basics without which there is no gospel. Jesus' Resurrection is a picture and promise of the resurrection of all believers.

1 Corinthians 16. Paul promised that he would soon come for a visit. He and some of the Corinthians would then take the offering they had been collecting to the needy Christians in Jerusalem.

2 CORINTHIANS

OVERVIEW

■ *2 Corinthians in a Nutshell. Second Corin-*
■ *thians is the most personal and one of the*
■ *most passionate of Paul's letters. Paul con-*
■ *trasted his own apostleship and his methods*
■ *of doing Christ's work with leaders who had*
■ *come to Corinth and sought to detract from*
■ *what Paul had done among the Corinthians.*
■ *The primary purpose of 2 Corinthians was to*
■ *prepare the church at Corinth for another*
■ *visit from Paul.*

Second Corinthians has three major sections:

2 Corinthians 1–7. This first major section of the letter focuses on Paul's relationship with the Corinthians. That relationship had been strained for a number of reasons, and Paul addressed these with a view toward reconciliation with the Corinthians. False apostles who claimed to be superior to Paul had impressed the Corinthians. Paul took this occasion to contrast his view of ministry and of the New Covenant itself with that of the false apostles. These chapters are a fascinating blend of the personal with theological truth that is stated simply and profoundly.

2 Corinthians 8–9. First Corinthians mentions the offering the Corinthians were collecting for the Christians in Jerusalem. In these chapters this theme reemerges. Paul encouraged liberal, sacrificial giving on their part. He used other Gentile churches as examples to encourage

Background. Paul is the author of this letter (1:1; 10:1). While it is a different kind of letter than Romans or even 1 Corianthians, it is characterized by his style. It contains more autobiographical material than any of his other writings. The letter is difficult to date, for we do not know the amount of time that separated 1 and 2 Corinthians. It has been variously dated between A.D. 55 and 57. The letter was penned at a difficult time between Paul and the Corinthians.

Ministering in Christ's name involves suffering as well as victory. Paul's references to his own sufferings show that even the most faithful followers of Christ endure sufferings. Although He sustains the Christian who suffers, God does not always deliver the Christian from suffering.

generosity. Churches of Macedonia, for instance, had given sacrificially and joyfully (8:1–5). Of course, pivotal to the whole matter of giving for others was the self-giving of Christ (8:9). Paul fully expected the Corinthians to give sacrificially, pointing out to them that they would be blessed in the process (9:6–15).

2 Corinthians 10–13. Paul returned to the subject of his relationship with the Corinthians and responded to the criticism that had been directed against him. They said he was bold when away from them but humble when present with them (10:1). Paul quoted them as saying, "His letters are weighty and forceful, but in person he is unimpressive and his speaking amounts to nothing" (10:10). By such criticisms Paul's opponents sought to undermine the strong relationship between Paul and the Corinthians.

Although his opponents' identity is uncertain, they preached another Jesus (11:4). They were "super-apostles" (11:5), evidently presenting themselves with rather forceful and impressive expressions as being much superior to Paul. Paul defended himself, being forced to boast of his own commitment, sacrifice, and service. Indeed, "the things that mark an apostle . . . were done among" them (12:12). In this way Paul defended the authenticity of his work and his apostleship. Despite the tough language arising out of obvious conflict, he closed his letter with a generous benediction, pronouncing grace, love, and fellowship upon them.

OVERVIEW

■ *Galatians in a Nutshell. Galatians is a pas-*
■ *sionate defense of the gospel not against*
■ *those who directly denied it but who sought*
■ *to add to it. Paul argued that the gospel is*
■ *sufficient and that to add to it is to under-*
■ *mine it.*

Background. There can be little doubt that the apostle Paul wrote the letter to the Galatians. This conclusion has seldom been called into question because the circumstances portrayed in the epistle, the details concerning Paul's life found in Galatians, and the theology of the book all coincide closely with information found in Acts and Paul's other letters. Galatians may have been written from Syrian Antioch in A.D. 48–49 or from Antioch, Corinth, Ephesus, or Macedonia in the early to mid–50s.

Paul faced two problems when he wrote Galatians. First, opponents attacked his authenticity as an apostle, and he wrote to defend his apostleship. Second, Paul's opponents preached a different gospel to the Galatians—a different gospel which some of the Galatian Christians followed (1:6). So Paul wrote to discredit their gospel and to defend the truth of the gospel of Christ.

Paul gave a fiery response to this disturbance. The Galatians were in danger of abandoning the gospel. In 1:1–5, Paul sent greetings to the churches, but he omitted the statement of praise or thanksgiving that normally follows. Paul was too disturbed to give thanks or praise. Instead, in 1:6–9, Paul expressed distress at their fickle faith. The Galatians had received the one and true gospel but were turning away from it. In one of the strongest warnings in the Scripture, Paul pronounced a curse on those who preached something different from the gospel he had preached to them.

The major portion of the epistle (1:10–6:10) can be divided into three parts:

Galatians 1:10–2:21. In this section Paul defended his qualifications as an apostle against the attacks of the Judaizers. What Paul taught and preached was not his opinion. It wasn't something he was taught by other humans. Christ Himself revealed this truth to Paul. When Paul met the Apostles in Jerusalem, they recognized and affirmed the truth of what Christ had revealed to Paul. This gospel is that both Jews and Gentiles are saved by the grace of God received by faith in Christ. The false teachers tried to convince the Galatians that, in addition to faith in Christ, Gentiles had to become Jews (and Gentile men circumcised) in order to be in right relationship with God.

Galatians 3:1–5:12. This section is the major argument of the epistle, where the differences between Paul's gospel and the Judaizers' heresy came to full light. Paul supported his thesis of faith alone on three principles: (1) the gift of the Spirit, (2) the promise and faith of Abraham, and (3) the curse of the Law.

The gift of the Spirit came to them through faith, not the Law. Abraham received the promise and righteousness by faith 430 years before the Law was given. People of faith were true children of Abraham and heirs of the promise. Because people did not keep the law when it came, they fell under its curse. The Law could only condemn sinners. Christ removed the curse of the Law. The Law was given as an interim provision until Christ came. Now He has come, and the believer is free. To turn back to the Law was to return to slavery.

Galatians 5:13–6:18. In this final section, Paul argued that freedom from the law doesn't give a person license to sin. Christian freedom required the believer to walk by the Spirit, which was contrary to the desires and works of the flesh. Those who walk by the Spirit will yield the fruit of the Spirit. We find Paul's teaching on the fruit of the Spirit in Galatians 5:22–23. Paul concluded his defense in 6:11–18, again urging them not to yield to circumcision and all it represented.

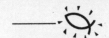

"But the fruit of the Spirit is love, joy, peace, patience, kindness, goodness, faithfulness, gentleness and self-control. Against such things there is no law" (Gal. 5:22–23).

EPHESIANS

OVERVIEW

■ *Ephesians in a Nutshell. Christ in His*
■ *Church and the Church in Christ is the*
■ *theme of Ephesians. Ephesians is also a man-*
■ *ual of Christian living. It pulls together much*
■ *of the material of the other letters of the New*
■ *Testament but in a more concise form. Ephe-*
■ *sians gives some practical advice for spiri-*
■ *tual growth and development.*

The letter has a salutation (1:1–2), two major sections (1:3–3:21 and 4:1–6:20), and a conclusion (6:21–24). A doxology (3:20–21) denotes the division between the two major sections, although both sections have some common themes.

Ephesians 1:13–3:21. Paul began by praising God for His grace in Christ. This grace was not an afterthought that God devised in response to Adam's sin. This has been God's plan from the beginning. God—Father, Son, and Holy Spirit—not only conceived the plan prior to Creation, but they are also ever at work to effect this plan. The key moment in this plan is Jesus' shedding His blood to provide forgiveness of sins and redemption from sin.

Jesus' death took place outside us. But His death takes effect in our lives as we hear and believe the gospel. At the same time, God's Spirit sets His seal on us, indicating that God now owns us and promises to carry out fully His purposes in us in time and eternity.

Background. The early church viewed Paul (1:1; 3:1) as author of Ephesians even though this letter contains a writing style, vocabulary, and even some teachings that are not typical of the apostle. Paul penned the letter while in prison (3:1; 4:1; 6:20). Paul most likely wrote Colossians, Philemon, and Philippians during the same imprisonment. It is plausible to suggest that Paul wrote the letter from Rome around A.D. 60–61. This would have transpired while Paul was housed in guarded rental quarters (Acts 28:30).

Before we heard and believed the gospel we were like dead people. Our sinful nature determined what we did, and we in ourselves were powerless to do otherwise. But God had mercy on us and did for us what we could never do for ourselves. By His merciful intervention we were made alive and given a whole new purpose for living.

God did this for both Jews and Gentiles. In Jesus' death, God broke down the wall of hostility that had long existed between these peoples. One by one, as persons are made alive in Christ, they are brought together in a magnificent building—a temple indwelt by God's Spirit.

Paul's glad task had been to bring this good news to the Gentiles. He now prayed that God's Spirit who dwelled with them would give them strength, that God's Spirit would increase their understanding and knowledge of God, and that they might experience and be filled with the love of God which goes beyond human understanding.

Ephesians 4:1–6:24. Paul looked at the practical implications of being in Christ. Ethical imperatives dominate the section. While believers are different and have diverse gifts, a unity binds them together—one body, one Spirit, one hope, one Lord, one faith, one baptism, and one God and Father.

Believers are called to a complete transformation which differs markedly from the lifestyles of unbelievers. Unbelievers—even the most noble—are characterized by an outlook that is ultimately futile. Unbelievers are blind to the most important realities in life, and so their attitudes and actions are out of touch with reality. The believer, on the other hand, becomes like

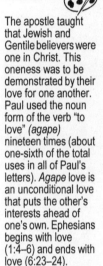

The apostle taught that Jewish and Gentile believers were one in Christ. This oneness was to be demonstrated by their love for one another. Paul used the noun form of the verb "to love" *(agape)* nineteen times (about one-sixth of the total uses in all of Paul's letters). *Agape* love is an unconditional love that puts the other's interests ahead of one's own. Ephesians begins with love (1:4–6) and ends with love (6:23–24).

God in holiness, purity, and righteousness. A central element of this is human speech, speaking the truth and saying that which helps build up others. Anger and malice must turn to love, compassion, and forgiveness.

"Walking in the light" means seeing what pleases God and doing it. Drunkenness from alcohol yields to being filled with God's Spirit which leads to praise and worship. Home life becomes as God originally intended. Wives relate to their husbands as to Christ. Husbands love their wives as Christ loved the church. Parents expect honor from children while training children in the Lord's way of love. Similarly, masters and servants respect and help one another.

To complete his letter, Paul called his readers to put on God's armor to avoid Satan's schemes. This leads to a life that seeks God's blessing for oneself, for other servants of God, and which is active in encouraging one's fellow believers.

OVERVIEW

- *Philippians in a Nutshell. Philippians is the*
- *most personal letter Paul wrote to a church.*

These were a people who loved Paul dearly and whom he loved. The letter from start to finish is characterized by joy. Paul rejoiced in the partnership he had with the Philippian Christians (1:4). The joy of partnership in the gospel rests on strong theological foundations.

As a highly personal letter, Philippians lacks the structure that some of Paul's letters have.

Philippians 1. The very thought of these believers in Philippi caused Paul to thank God for them. They were precious to him, and he longed to see them. Because he loved them so, he prayed for their continued growth in Christ (vv. 3–11). He wanted them to know about his situation as a prisoner of Rome (vv. 12–26). His captors were being evangelized (vv. 12–13). His compatriots had gained confidence through his bold example (v. 14). Even the brethren who were working with wrong motives were sharing the good news actively. Paul rejoiced in their work (vv. 15–18). Paul seemed to be hopeful about being released and being reunited with the Philippians, but he did convey to them that he had looked death straight in the eye and was not afraid of it. After all, death would bring him into the full presence of Christ. The downside of death was that, for a time, Paul would be

Background.
Philippians was written while the apostle Paul was in prison, probably from Rome about A.D. 62.

separated from the Philippians and could not do for them what he would like.

Philippians 2. When Paul returned to Philippi, he hoped to find a church united in Christ. Philippians 1:27–4:9 is a multifaceted call for unity in the church. The great cause of the proclamation of the gospel called for them to be united in spirit, in task, and in confidence (1:27–30). Their common Christian experience (2:1) and purpose (2:2) should also rule out a self-centered, self-serving attitude (2:3–4). Those who follow Christ must follow Him in selfless service to others (2:5–11).

Paul was concerned that the Philippians demonstrate the reality of their Christian profession in action. Neither the grumbling so characteristic of Israel in the wilderness nor the perversity of a world that does not know God should characterize the church.

Philippians 3. The tone of the letter changes in chapter 3. The encouragement to rejoice (v. 1) unexpectedly becomes a stern warning (v. 2). A problem was threatening the church at Philippi, which had the potential of destroying the foundation of unity and the basis of joy. The exact nature of the problem is unclear. Jewish legalism (vv. 2–11), Christian or Gnostic perfectionism (vv. 12–16), and pagan libertinism (vv. 17–21) are all attacked.

What is clear, however, is that Paul countered the heretical teachings with Christian truths: Jesus Christ is the only avenue to righteousness (vv. 2–11); the stature of Christ is the goal of Christian maturity (vv. 12–16); and the nature of Christ and His kingdom are the standards by which the Christian must live (vv. 17–21).

Philippians 2:6–11 is known as the *kenosis* passage (from the Greek word translated "emptied" in 2:7 RSV). The language and structure of the passage have convinced most commentators that Paul was quoting a hymn which was already in use in the church. The purpose of the pre-Pauline hymn was probably to teach the believer about the nature and work of Christ. Preexistence, Incarnation, Passion, Resurrection, and Exaltation are all summarized in a masterful fashion. In the context of Philippians, however, the *kenosis* passage is used to highlight the humility and selfless service demonstrated by Jesus, whose example the Christian is to follow.

Philippians 4. Chapter 4 returns to a more positive instruction and affirmation of the church. Two women, Euodias and Syntyche (vv. 2–3), were exhorted to end their conflict, for personal disagreements may be as damaging to the unity of the church as false doctrine.

COLOSSIANS

OVERVIEW

- *Colossians in a Nutshell. This short letter*
- *sets forth the supremacy and sufficiency of*
- *Christ. Paul was writing to a context*
- *where Christ was proclaimed but He was*
- *seen as only part of God's revelation and*
- *plan for redemption. Paul asserted that*
- *when a person has Christ he has the very*
- *fullness of God.*

Background. Tradition supports the letter's claim that Paul was the author (Col. 1:1). Paul had never been to Colosse, but he wrote to them to address matters raised by Epaphras (1:7). The letter would have been written about the same time as Ephesians and Philemon (around A.D. 60–61).

Colossians may be divided into two main parts. The first part (1–2) is a polemic against false teachings. The second part (3–4) is made up of exhortations to proper Christian living. The introduction (1:1–2) is in the form of a Hellenistic, personal letter. The senders (Paul and Timothy) and the recipients (the Colossian church) are identified, and a greeting is expressed (the usual Pauline "grace and peace" replaced the usual secular "greeting").

Colossians 1:3–2:23. Typical of Paul, a lengthy thanksgiving (1:3–8) and prayer (1:9–14) lead into the body of the letter. Paul thanked God for the faith, hope, and love (1:4–5) which the Colossians had by virtue of their positive response to the gospel. He prayed that they might have a full knowledge and understanding of God's will and lead a life worthy of redeemed saints, citizens of the kingdom of Christ (1:9–14).

The doctrinal section that follows begins with a description of the grandeur of the preeminent

Christ (1:15–20). Though the precise meaning of some words and phrases is uncertain, there is no doubt as to Paul's intent. He meant to present Jesus as fully God incarnate (1:15, 19), as supreme Lord over all creation (1:15, 17), as supreme Lord of the church (1:18), and as the only Source of reconciliation (1:20).

Colossians 3–4. The last two chapters of Colossians exhort believers to live out the new life made possible by Christ's work of redemption set forth in the first two chapters. The command to "put to death" (3:5) and to "rid yourselves of all such things" (3:8) which will reap the wrath of God (3:5–11) is balanced by the command to "clothe yourselves with" (3:12) those things characteristic of God's chosen people (3:12–17). However, the changes are far from superficial. They stem from the Christian's new nature and submission to the rule of Christ in every area of one's life (3:9, 10, 15–17).

Rules for the household appear in 3:18–4:1. The typical first-century household is assumed, thus the passage addresses wives and husbands, fathers and children, masters and slaves. Paul's concern was that the structures as they existed be governed by Christian principles. Submission to the Lord (3:18, 20, 22; 4:1), Christian love (3:19), and the prospect of divine judgment (3:24–4:1) must determine the way people treat one another regardless of their social station. This Christian motivation distinguishes these house rules from those that can be found in Jewish and pagan sources.

A final group of exhortations (4:2–6) and an exchange of greetings (4:7–17) bring the letter to a close. Notable in this final section are: (1) the mention of Onesimus (4:9), which links this

Colossians

Becoming and being a Christian. Being Christian continues on the same basis as we began, faith in Christ. Christ reveals Himself to us, changes us, delivers us, and leads us only in response to our continued trust. Our response is to answer His love and faithfulness with our own.

letter with Philemon; (2) the mention of a letter at Laodicea (4:16), which may have been Ephesians; and (3) Paul's concluding signature which indicates that the letter was prepared by an *amanuensis* (secretary) (4:18).

50

1 THESSALONIANS

OVERVIEW

- **1 Thessalonians in a Nutshell.** *Having*
- *received a report that they were growing in*
- *their faith, Paul wrote this letter to answer*
- *the Thessalonians' questions and to defend*
- *himself against enemies who were spreading*
- *false rumors. One key theme of the letter is*
- *the return of Christ.*

The letter has two major sections: chapters 1–3 and 4–5.

1 Thessalonians 1–3. In this first major section, Paul expressed thankfulness for and reassurance toward the Thessalonians. He gave thanks for the Thessalonians' faithfulness (1:3–10). In fact, they had become models for believers in Macedonia and Achaia (1:7), turning from idols to "serve the living and true God" (1:9) and to await the coming of Christ from heaven (1:10).

1 Thessalonians 4–5. Among the problems the Thessalonian church faced were persecution by pagans (2:14) and a temptation for believers to accept pagan sexual standards (4:4–8). Some of the Christians seem to have given up working and to have relied on others to supply their needs (4:11–12). There was uncertainty about the fate of believers who had died, and some of the Thessalonians appear to have thought that Christ would come back soon and take them all to be with Him. What would happen to those who had died before the great event (4:13–18)? Paul's reply to this gives us information about

Background.
Galatians probably was the first of Paul's letters to be written, and 1 Thessalonians was the second. Paul traveled to Thessalonica, the capital city of Macedonia, on his second missionary journey around A.D. 51. Luke reported the brief visit, Paul's preaching ministry there with Silas, and the subsequent persecution that drove them out of the city (Acts 17:1–9). Many people believed in Jesus Christ before the missionaries were compelled to leave. From Thessalonica, Paul went to Berea, Athens, and then Corinth. Timothy and Silas, who had been with Paul at Thessalonica, rejoined Paul in Corinth (Acts 18:5; 1 Thess. 3:6). Paul wrote 1 Thessalonians in response to Timothy's report shortly after his arrival.

The nature of the Second Coming. We sorrow when loved ones die but with the assurance that death for a believer is only being "away from the body and at home with the Lord" (2 Cor. 5:8). In God's own time we will all be together eternally in the glorious family of God and "so we will be with the Lord forever" (1 Thess. 4:17).

Christ's return that we find nowhere else. Again, some of the believers seem to have been concerned about the time of Jesus' return (5:1–11). So Paul wrote this pastoral letter to meet the needs of inexperienced Christians and to bring them closer to Christ.

OVERVIEW

- *2 Thessalonians in a Nutshell. After learning*
- *that the believers at Thessalonica were*
- *unclear about what Paul had previously*
- *taught about future events, he wrote this let-*
- *ter to provide them a fuller explanation. He*
- *covered the topics of Christ's return and the*
- *"day of the Lord" (2:2). Because of the teach-*
- *ing of some, several members mistakenly*
- *believed that their persecution was the tribu-*
- *lation about which Paul had spoken. Paul*
- *corrected their misunderstanding.*

Background. Paul's authorship of 2 Thessalonians has had extremely strong support throughout church history. The interval between 1 and 2 Thessalonians must have been rather short, for the second epistle does not presuppose major changes in the inner constitution of the Thessalonian church or in the conditions under which Paul was writing.

2 Thessalonians 1. Following a brief introduction (vv. 1–2), Paul explained his prayer concerns for his readers. He expressed thanksgiving for their growth in faith and love for one another in spite of their intense sufferings (vv. 3–5). He assured his readers that he prayed constantly that their way of living would ensure God's final commendation of their actions and life purpose (vv. 11–12).

2 Thessalonians 2. Paul then focused on the topic of Christ's return. He used the term "day of the Lord" (v. 2) to describe the complex events that will occur at Jesus' return. He assured the Thessalonians that these events had not yet begun even though someone had used devious methods to suggest that the events were already unfolding (vv. 1–2). Paul insisted that a large-scale rebellion against God and the appearance of the man of lawlessness would occur before the day of the Lord comes

(vv. 3–4). This man of lawlessness will demand worship as God, work counterfeit miracles, and inspire all types of evil in his followers (vv. 5, 9–10). Those who follow him will face condemnation because they loved wickedness and accepted lies rather than divine truth (vv. 11–12). The display of power by the man of lawlessness will increase after the restrainer is removed (v. 7). Jesus will render this lawless one utterly powerless at His return.

Paul expressed gratitude for God's work among the Thessalonians and anticipated a glorious spiritual future for them (vv. 13–17). He urged them to stand firm in their obedience to the teaching he had given them, and he prayed for God to encourage them to fulfill that purpose.

2 Thessalonians 3. Paul expressed some final concerns. He was concerned about three needs in the Thessalonian church (vv. 1–15). After requesting prayer for his own ministry and protection (a true demonstration of spiritual humility!), Paul expressed confidence that his readers would persevere in their obedience (vv. 1–5). A second concern involved inappropriate conduct by some of the believers. Paul urged the Thessalonians to avoid a habit of idleness, to settle into productive labor, and to earn their own living (vv. 6–13). His third concern involved the outwardly disobedient. He urged the church to administer firm but sensitive discipline to those who rebelled against his teaching (vv. 14–15).

Not even the anticipation of Christ's return should lead Christians away from work. People able to work should earn their daily bread. Believers are to be exemplary in work, doing it as unto the Lord.

Paul concluded this letter by reminding his readers that only divine strength would allow them to accomplish the goals he had set before them. He closed with a personal greeting and provided a sign of authenticity for his letter.

1 TIMOTHY

OVERVIEW

- 1 Timothy in a Nutshell. Paul encouraged
- Timothy in his ministry in Ephesus, urging
- him to remain faithful and giving him
- instruction about dealing with false doctrine
- and matters of church organization and
- administration.

Background. Paul's three letters to Timothy and Titus are called the Pastoral Letters. These letters were written near the end of Paul's life, between A.D. 64 and 67, to guide his two younger associates.

After the salutation, Paul admonished Timothy to be responsible for seeing that teachers reject heresy and teach sound doctrine (1:3–20). Elements of church organization then received attention (2:1–3:13), followed by further instructions pertaining to Timothy's leadership of the church (3:14–6:19). Paul closed the letter with final instruction to Timothy and a benediction (6:20–21).

Paul's first letter to Timothy breaks according to its chapters:

1 Timothy 1. Paul wrote as an apostle of Jesus Christ with the authority of Christ.

He urged Timothy to deal forthrightly with false teaching in the church at Ephesus. The error described in verses 3–4 was Jewish in nature. Some were falsely teaching a mythological treatment of Old Testament genealogies. This teaching was generating a lot of meaningless controversy. Timothy was urged to teach "sound doctrine" in its place (vv. 10–11).

1 Timothy 2. Paul showed the priority of prayer in the worship services in the church. Seven

different Greek words appear in the New Testament for prayer, and four of them occur in verse 1. One of the most significant statements in the entire New Testament is found in verse 5. Paul wrote that there is "one God" and "one mediator between God and men, the man Christ Jesus." Monotheism is clearly taught as opposed to the polytheism of the first-century religious world. *Mediator* is a word that means "go-between." Jesus is humanity's "go-between" to God. He is also called our "ransom" in verse 6. A ransom was paid to a slave owner to purchase the freedom of the slave. Jesus paid for our redemption with His death on the cross.

Today's church is to seek as leaders persons ready to walk the high road spiritually and morally.

1 Timothy 3. Paul explained the qualifications for church leadership in this chapter. Fifteen moral and ethical requirements are mentioned in verses 2–7.

1 Timothy 4. Paul affirms that "everything God created is good" (v. 4). Some false teachers maintained that marriage and certain foods were wrong. Paul drew from the message of Genesis in which God affirmed that everything He created was good! It is man who takes God's good creation and corrupts it. The apostle reminded Timothy to be a "good minister of Christ Jesus" (v. 6) and to "set an example for the believers in speech, in life, in love, in faith and in purity" (v. 12).

1 Timothy 5. Paul gave practical instructions concerning the ministry of the church to various groups that comprised its membership.

1 Timothy 6. The teachers of false doctrine were motivated by "financial gain" (v. 5). Paul warned, in light of this fact and others, that "the love of money is a root of all kinds of evil" (v. 10).

OVERVIEW

- 2 Timothy in a Nutshell. Paul urged Timothy
- to be faithful, to endure the difficulties, and
- to fulfill his calling as a preacher of the gos-
- pel. He foresaw the end of his own mission-
- ary career in martyrdom (4:6–8). The
- situation was made more difficult by
- Demas's desertion of the missionary enter-
- prise (4:10) and by Alexander the copper-
- smith, who hurt Paul deeply (4:14).

Background. This may well have been Paul's last letter. The letter contains Paul's stirring words of encouragement and instruction to his young disciple. Paul longed to see Timothy (1:4) and asked him to come to Rome for a visit. It is generally believed that Timothy went.

Paul's second letter to Timothy breaks easily according to its chapters:

2 Timothy 1. Paul reminded Timothy of his heritage in the faith—a faith that first lived in his grandmother Lois and in his mother Eunice (v. 5). Paul had become Timothy's father in the ministry (v. 2). Timothy may have been a naturally timid person. Because of this, Paul told him to minister with "a spirit of power" (v. 7). The Holy Spirit empowers believers, but we should be careful to exercise this power in a "spirit . . . of love and of self-discipline" (v. 7). Two men, Phygelus and Hermogenes, deserted Paul (v. 15). Onesiphorus was a refreshing friend and not ashamed of Paul's chains (v. 16).

2 Timothy 2. Paul urged Timothy to be strong in Jesus Christ. Paul used the metaphors of a good soldier, athlete, and a hard-working farmer when describing the Christian's calling. The purpose of that calling is so all "may obtain the salvation that is in Christ Jesus" (v. 10). Timothy was to be one who "correctly handles the word of truth" (v. 15) in the face of those who mishandled it. Hymenaeus (1 Tim. 1:20) and Philetus were singled out. They were teaching that the resurrection had already taken place and were destroying the faith of some (v. 18).

2 Timothy 3. Paul's reference to "the last days" was a reference to the Second Coming of Jesus. The days preceding His return will be "terrible" (v. 1). Characteristics of these last days have appeared in many different ages, but the times before Jesus' actual return will be even more intense. Paul listed eighteen characteristics of evil men in verses 2–5. He compared them to Jannes and Jambres who opposed Moses (v. 8). Although these two individuals are not mentioned in the Old Testament, Jewish tradition maintains that these men were two Egyptian magicians who opposed Moses and Aaron. The evil and false teaching is to be overcome by Holy Scripture (vv. 16–17).

2 Timothy 4. Paul further instructed Timothy to be prepared to "preach the Word" (v. 2) at all times. The need is paramount, for people will not always adhere to "sound doctrine" (v. 3). Paul, drawing on the imagery of Numbers 28:24, compared his life to that of a "drink offering" (v. 6). This was poured on a sacrifice before it was offered. He was ready to depart this life and to go to be with the Lord. He anticipated the "crown of righteousness" that awaited him (v. 8). Paul closed the letter with practical instructions and pastoral remarks for Timothy.

TITUS

OVERVIEW

Background. There is good evidence that Paul was released from his first imprisonment at Rome. Between this and his last imprisonment, Paul and Titus worked on Crete, leading many to faith in Christ. This letter to Titus was written in the mid 60s.

■ *Titus in a Nutshell. Paul had left Titus in*
■ *Crete to complete the work begun there. This*
■ *is a follow-up letter to Titus giving him*
■ *encouragement and specific instructions.*

Summary of Contents

Titus 1. Titus's first duty was to appoint elders. The qualifications listed in verses 6–9 are similar to those mentioned in 1 Timothy 3:1–7. False teachers threatened the church. He mentioned the "circumcision group" (v. 10), a reference to converts to the Christian faith from Judaism who apparently taught that the rite of circumcision was necessary to be a complete Christian. This group of teachers and all who sought to lead the people astray were corrupt in their minds and detestable in their actions (vv. 15–16).

Titus 2. Paul urged Titus to teach "sound doctrine" (v. 1) to correct the false teaching. Proper teaching will lead to proper conduct in the lives of believers. Titus was to be an example to all (v. 7). His teaching was to be characterized by "integrity," "seriousness," and a "soundness of speech" (vv. 7–8), so that the false teachers could "have nothing bad to say about us" (v. 8). A transformed life is evidence of receiving God's grace and salvation. The anticipation of the return of Christ is called "the blessed hope" (v. 13). The hope of His return should motivate us to godly living.

Titus 3. Paul reminded believers "to be subject to rulers and authorities" (v. 1). The subjection is to be voluntary because the institution of government was created by God. Believers ought to treat all persons with consideration and humility. Paul reminded them of their past and of God's kindness and love. His kindness and love "appeared" (v. 4). Our salvation is not because of "righteous things we had done, but because of his mercy" (v. 5). Salvation is likened to the "washing of rebirth and renewal by the Holy Spirit" (v. 5). The washing of rebirth is a metaphor of a divine inner act. This act is symbolized by believer's baptism. Renewal refers to the "making new" by the Holy Spirit.

Paul concluded the letter with some practical instructions for Titus. Zenas, the lawyer, and Apollos probably delivered the letter to Titus (v. 13).

PHILEMON

OVERVIEW

- *Philemon in a Nutshell. Paul wrote to*
- *Philemon, telling him that his runaway*
- *slave, Onesimus, had come to faith in Christ.*
- *Paul urged Philemon to forgive Onesimus*
- *and accept him back as a brother in Christ.*

Paul's only epistle of a private and personal nature that is included in the New Testament was written to Philemon in A.D. 61. Philemon's slave, Onesimus, had robbed him and escaped to Rome. There under the preaching of Paul, Onesimus came to faith in Christ. Paul wrote to Philemon concerning Onesimus and sent the letter along with Onesimus back to Philemon in Colosse. Paul asked Philemon to forgive and receive Onesimus not as a slave but as a brother (v.16). This request was not made from Paul's apostolic authority but tenderly as a Christian friend. Paul wrote, "Welcome him as you would welcome me" (v.17).

Paul also stated that he was willing to pay any damages caused by Onesimus. Some scholars indicate that Paul may have been asking subtly that Philemon release Onesimus so that he could return and aid Paul in his evangelistic endeavors. Philemon had a judicial right to punish severely or even kill Onesimus. Paul's short epistle of some 355 Greek words challenged Philemon to apply Christian love in dealing with Onesimus.

Background. Philemon is closely linked with the Epistle to the Colossians. The letter was carried by Onesimus to Philemon with Tychicus (Col. 4:7–9; Eph. 6:21–22). The letter was written near the end of Paul's first Roman imprisonment at the same time as Ephesians and Colossians, about A.D. 60–61.

OVERVIEW

Background. The book of Hebrews is anonymous in that the name of the author is not mentioned in the book. The original readers knew who the writer was, but he remains unknown to us. Two strong reasons for believing the letter was written prior to A.D. 70 are (1) the destruction of the Temple isn't mentioned, and (2) the Temple is spoken of in the present tense.

■ *Hebrews in a Nutshell. The writer of*
■ *Hebrews presented Jesus Christ as the High*
■ *Priest who offered Himself as the perfect sac-*
■ *rifice for sins (8:1–2; 10:11–18). Christ is*
■ *the fulfillment of and so was superior to*
■ *every aspect of Old Testament religion. The*
■ *writer pressed this truth to prevent his read-*
■ *ers from abandoning Christ and returning to*
■ *Judaism (10:26–29).*

The writer of Hebrews presented Christ as superior to the Old Testament prophets, angels, Moses, Joshua, and Aaron. He laced magnificent discussions of Christ's person and work into frightening passages warning against apostasy (1:1–2:4). The superiority of Christ led the writer to appeal for faith (chap. 11), stamina (12:3–11), and good works (13:16).

Whether the recipients were Jewish or Gentile Christians, the writer saw a clear and present danger. The writer's response was to point to the superiority of Jesus:

Hebrews 1:1–4. Jesus is God's supreme revelation.

Hebrews 1:5–2:18. Jesus is superior to the angels.

Hebrews 3:1–4:13. Jesus is superior to Moses.

Hebrews 4:14–10:18. Jesus is superior to the earthly high priest. He has a superior ministry that establishes a superior covenant that is able to bring to maturity those who have faith.

Hebrews 10:19–12:29. The writer encouraged the practice of spiritual endurance.

Hebrews 13:1–25. The writer closed with final exhortations.

Because of the Jesus' superiority, the writer exhorted his readers not to neglect such a great salvation (2:3). They should enter God's rest while it is still available (4:1–13); they should go on to maturity (6:1–8). Because Jesus' high priesthood is superior and because He has a superior ministry that establishes a superior covenant, the readers should draw near God's throne in confidence (10:19–25).

The writer of Hebrews also confronted directly the recipients' fear of suffering. He believed that God's children suffer because they are His children (12:7–8). Suffering functions as a discipline that leads God's children to maturity or perfection. Jesus was perfected in this way (2:10; 5:8) and was qualified to stand in God's presence in the heavenly sanctuary as High Priest (2:17–18; 5:9–10).

"We cry too often to be delivered from the punishment, instead of the sin that lies behind it. We are anxious to escape from the things that cause us pain rather than from the things that cause God pain"—G. Campbell Morgan, from Warren W. Wiersbe, *With the Word* (Nashville: Oliver Nelson, 1991), 822.

Thus, just as Jesus learned what it meant to be obedient to God through suffering (5:8), the readers were exhorted to exhibit the same kind of obedience in their suffering (10:36–39). "Shrinking back" from God in the face of suffering is a sin that God detests (3:12–19; 10:26–31). Jesus was tempted (2:18; 5:7) but did not sin (4:15). Because Jesus remained faithful and did not sin during the hour of His suffering, He became the source of eternal salvation for all who obey Him.

The writer also encouraged the recipients to remain faithful in the midst of suffering by giving them examples of others who were able to remain faithful (11:1–39). The writer reminded them of their own past faithfulness in suffering (10:32–39) and of the example of their former leaders (13:7). Those who remain obedient to God in the midst of suffering are able to do so by means of their faith.

JAMES

OVERVIEW

- *James in a Nutshell. James wrote to Jewish*
- *Christians facing trials and persecution.*
- *Under the threat of persecution, the readers*
- *considered compromising their Christian*
- *commitment and accommodating themselves*
- *to pre-Christian patterns. James spoke as a*
- *pastor to urge his friends to develop spiritual*
- *stamina in facing persecution. He also spoke*
- *as a prophet to urge those who considered*
- *compromise to give evidence of their faith.*

Background. The traditional view is that James, the half brother of Jesus, is the author of this letter. James was not a believer until after Jesus' Resurrection. One of the Lord's Resurrection appearances was to his brother James. What we know about James and his speech in Acts 15 are consistent with the content and background of this letter. The letter is variously dated from the mid-forties to the early sixties, just before James' death.

Patience in the wake of trials and temptations is the subject both of the introduction and of the conclusion of the letter, but finding a single theme that ties together the warnings and commands of James is difficult. At times James reflected the attitude of a compassionate pastor as he shepherded his flock through trials (1:1–18). At other times he wrote with the fire of an Old Testament prophet as he warned, denounced, and called for changed behavior (1:19–27; 4:1–12). It is best to view James as a loose collection of messages or homilies that deal with various subjects.

James 1:1–18. A first step in dealing with a trial is to see it as an opportunity for growth. God stands ready to give wisdom for walking through trials, but we must ask in faith rather than doubt. God doesn't tempt human beings. He doesn't lure people to do evil. God is perfectly good, and His goodness never changes.

"If anyone thinks himself to be religious and yet does not bridle his tongue but deceives his own heart, this man's religion is worthless." (James 1:27, NASB).

James 1:19–27. God's people are not only to hear God's Word but also to put it into practice. And they are to be careful how they use words.

James 2:1–13. Partiality must be avoided in the family of faith.

James 2:14–26. Faith inevitably expresses itself in good works. Claiming faith which isn't productive of good works may be self-deception.

James 3. James returned to the importance of the tongue. The tongue is small but powerful. It is exceedingly difficult to control.

James 4. The Christian needs to be alert for jealously and pride.

James 5:1–6. Wealthy people need to remind themselves often of the dangers of wealth to their spiritual well-being.

James 5:7–12. Patience is of great value in the Christian life. It needs to be cultivated.

James 5:13–18. Bringing our needs before God and confessing our sins are important disciplines that will keep us close to the Lord.

James 5:19–20. Those who bring back straying Christians are doing something with far-reaching consequences.

1 PETER

OVERVIEW

- 1 Peter in a Nutshell. *Peter encouraged his*
- *readers in the Christian life, offering them*
- *hope as they faced suffering that comes with*
- *being a follower of Christ.*

To accomplish this, Peter urged all Christians to obey their leaders, servants to be subject to their masters, and husbands and wives to demonstrate honor and submission to one another. The vivid descriptions of Christ's suffering and death (2:21–25; 3:18) could serve as an encouragement for Christians to conquer evil and endure to the end.

1 Peter 1:1–12. Christians have a substantial hope of eternal life that puts into perspective the sufferings of the present time. This hope was foreseen by the prophets.

1 Peter 1:13–2:3. Peter called on his readers to conduct their lives in light of this hope. They were to put aside attitudes and behavior that characterized their former life. They were to be sincere.

1 Peter 2:4–10. Christians are to realize that they are now God's people and to live accordingly.

1 Peter 2:11–3:12. Christians are to respect all authority. When they suffer unjustly, they are to remember how Jesus responded to undeserved suffering and respond the way He did. Wives are to be more concerned about purity of heart

Background. The letter of 1 Peter was written to Jewish and Christian believers living in the northern part of Asia Minor. They faced persecution because of their commitment to Christ. Peter wrote to urge them to show stamina and commitment. Peter also wanted his readers to show a Christian lifestyle that would convert pagan sneers and accusations into appreciation and respect.

than outward appearance. Husbands are to honor their wives and treat them with care.

1 Peter 3:13–4:19. Peter prepared his readers not to be surprised at having to suffer as followers of Christ. He reminded them that God sees clearly all that happens and that time is short. God will bring justice. In light of this, they are to live disciplined lives.

1 Peter 5:1–9. Leaders are to take Christ as their model. They are to put the good of their people above their own interests.

1 Peter 5:10–14. Peter closed with praises to God and greetings to the church.

"A man may be perfected through suffering or be made worse through suffering, it depends on his disposition"—Oswald Chambers.

2 PETER

OVERVIEW

■ *2 Peter in a Nutshell. Peter felt strongly that*
■ *his death was near (1:14–15). He wanted to*
■ *leave a spiritual testament that would pro-*
■ *vide helpful instruction after his departure.*
■ *He provided warning against the character*
■ *and false teaching of heretics who would*
■ *infiltrate the church (2:1–19; 3:1–4). To*
■ *provide protection against their errors, he*
■ *urged Christians to develop proper virtues*
■ *(1:3–11) and to grow constantly in God's*
■ *grace (3:17–18).*

The following examines Peter's letter according to its chapters:

2 Peter 1. Peter urged his readers to grow in the virtues of faith, goodness, knowledge, self-control, perseverance, godliness, kindness, and love (2 Pet. 1:5–9). Growing Christians will not be susceptible to heretical influence. Believers must continually give attention to the Word of God.

2 Peter 2. Peter described the moral errors of the heretics.

2 Peter 3. Peter exposed their doctrinal error in the denial of Jesus' return. He concluded with an appeal for growth as an antidote to pernicious heresy.

Peter emphasized practical Christian living by the motifs of growth by addition (1:3–8); judgment (3:11–14); and exhortation to growth

Background. Second Peter differs in a number of important ways from 1 Peter. These differences have led many to conclude that Peter didn't write both. One possible explanation of the differences is that Peter dictated 1 Peter to Silas who then wrote in his own style. Second Peter was written entirely by Peter. If this is the case, 2 Peter was written in Rome between A.D. 64 and 66. The brevity of the letter resulted in its being ignored for centuries by the church. Few Christians made use of it until the time of Origen (A.D. 250).

Second Peter stresses the importance and reliability of Scripture. It is God's message and must be heeded, even when it is difficult to understand. Understanding Scripture comes through the same Spirit who inspired its writing. One of the strongest statements in the Bible about its own reliability and inspiration is found in 1:20–21.

(3:17–18). The Word of God holds the forefront of this short letter:

- Chapter 1 emphasizes knowledge (vv. 3, 5, 6, 8, 12, 20–21) and its divine origin.
- Chapter 2 shows its historicity (vv. 4–8).
- Chapter 3 indicates that Paul's letters are equal with "the other Scriptures" (vv.15–16).

Peter held to a high view of Scripture (1:19–21), and he viewed Paul's writings as "Scripture" (3:16). He designated Jesus Christ as "Savior" and "Lord" (1:1–2), and he outlined his observation of Jesus' Transfiguration (1:16–18). He affirmed the return of Christ (3:1–4) and asserted God's sovereign control of the events of history (3:13). He used the certainty of Christ's return as an incentive to appeal for godly living (3:14).

1 JOHN

OVERVIEW

- 1 John in a Nutshell. John wrote to
- strengthen the joy (1:4) of his readers and to
- give them assurance of their relationship
- with Jesus Christ (5:13). He also wanted to
- prepare them for dealing with false teachers
- (4:1–3).

The epistle of 1 John presents three criteria for testing the Christian profession of teachers and individual Christians. First, professing Christians need to present righteousness as the right behavior (2:3–4). Second, they must demonstrate love as the correct attitude of Christian living (4:8). Third, they need to hold to the correct view of Christ as the proper teaching of Christians (4:3). Those who demonstrate these three traits have eternal life. John would repeat these three themes several times in the letter as tests to determine the presence of eternal life.

First John is difficult to outline because its theme recurs throughout the letter. Outlines with varying numbers of divisions have been suggested for 1 John. For example, the simple structure below is based on the repetition of the statement "God is," found three times in the letter:

- "God is light" (1:5).
- God "is righteous" (2:29).
- "God is love" (4:8).

First John demands that these qualities must dominate the lives of believers.

Background. Leaders in the early church assumed that John the apostle wrote this letter although the author never identified himself by name. Church fathers Polycarp, Irenaeus, and Tertullian all argued for apostolic authorship of this epistle.

"If we claim to be without sin, we deceive ourselves and the truth is not in us. If we confess our sins, he is faithful and just and will forgive us our sins and purify us from all unrighteousness" (1 John 1:8–9).

1 John 1:1–2:28. As a way of refuting the false teaching that threatened the community, John quoted tenets of the opponents and answered each point. He called those who remained not only to claim that they live in the light but also to do those things which constitute living in the light (2:3–11). The elder gave assurance to the community and warned believers that they could not practice love for one another and love for the world at the same time (2:15–17). "The world" here means all that is opposed to Christ. Dissension had already split the community, and the elder warned those who remained about the dangers of the false teaching (2:18–27).

1 John 2:29–4:7. One of the tests of faithfulness is righteousness (2:29). The opponents may have emphasized the present realization of the church's hope for the future, saying that the judgment was already past and Christians had already passed from death into life. Hope for the future, however, carries with it the imperative of righteous, purified living. Christians cannot make sin a way of life (cp. 3:6, 9 with 1:8–10).

1 John 4:8–5:21. Another test of faithfulness is living by the command to love one another, which means sharing with those in need (3:11–24, esp. v. 17). The false prophets, who had gone out from the community, denied the Incarnation (4:1–6). The Incarnation is crucial for Christian doctrine, however, because in Christ we find the love of God revealed (4:7–21). Love of God requires that we love one another.

John advocated the genuineness of Christ's humanity (1:1–2) and called those who questioned the reality of Jesus' Incarnation "antichrists"

(4:1–3). He presented the death of Christ as an atoning sacrifice for sins (2:2), and he taught the return of Christ (2:28). He denied the idea that Christians can make a practice of sinning (3:8–9), and he called for a demonstration of the reality of faith by ministry (3:16–18).

John opposed Docetism, the denial of the reality of Christ's body, by teaching that he had heard, seen, and touched Christ (1:1). He also emphasized that the same Jesus Christ appeared at both the baptism and the Crucifixion (5:6).

OVERVIEW

■ *2 John in a Nutshell. John mentioned twin*
■ *themes in writing 2 John. First, he urged his*
■ *readers to practice love with one another*
■ *(2 John 5). Second, he called them to prac-*
■ *tice truth in affirming the correct doctrine*
■ *about Jesus (2 John 7–11).*

Summary of Contents

2 John 1–3. Second John was written by the elder to "the elect lady" who could be a specific woman or a sister church.

2 John 4–6. John praised the lady for following the truth and appealed for her to continue to show love.

2 John 7–13. His real concern was to warn "the elect lady" about those "who do not acknowledge Jesus Christ as coming in the flesh" (v. 7). Such deceivers and antichrists are not to be received by the church. These were apparently members of the same group referred to in 1 John 2:19 and 4:1–2.

3 JOHN

OVERVIEW

■ *3 John in a Nutshell. This letter presents a*
■ *contrast between the truth and service dem-*
■ *onstrated by Gaius and the arrogance shown*
■ *by Diotrephes. John emphasized that "truth"*
■ *is a kind of behavior that agrees with the*
■ *doctrine Christians profess (3 John 8). The*
■ *autocratic behavior of Diotrephes violated*
■ *this behavior. John wanted to bring his dom-*
■ *ineering practices to an end.*

3 John 1–8. Third John is a personal letter from the elder to Gaius, who had been providing hospitality to fellow Christians and messengers from John's community.

3 John 9–11. John rebuked the domineering Diotrephes for his dictatorial practices.

3 John 12–14. John praised Demetrius (v. 12), who probably carried the letter.

Background. There is little evidence for the use of 3 John before the third century. The brevity and lack of a specific address for the letter would have contributed to its neglect. Eusebius classified the letter among the disputed writings of the New Testament, but the church came to accept it as a product of the apostle John.

JUDE

OVERVIEW

Background. The author identified himself as "a servant of Jesus Christ and a brother of James" (v. 1). In presenting himself as a brother of the Lord's half brother (James 1:1), he modestly neglected to mention his own relationship to Jesus (Matt. 13:55; Mark 6:3). He was initially an unbeliever (John 7:3–5), but in writing this epistle, he displayed a vigorous faith.

■ *Jude in a Nutshell. Jude began with the inten-*
■ *tion of discussing the theme of salvation.*
■ *Awareness of the infiltration of false teachers*
■ *led Jude to depart from his original plan.*
■ *First, he warned against and condemned*
■ *false teachers. Second, he urged his readers*
■ *to greater firmness and commitment.*

Jude 3–4. Jude wanted to write about the salvation he shared with his readers, but a more urgent matter arose. The truth of the gospel was being challenged.

Jude 5–16. Those who undermine the truth are like the unfaithful Israelites who rebelled against God in the wilderness.

Jude 17–23. Jude said believers should not be surprised at these attacks on truth. This has been prophesied. Rather, this is a call to take care how one lives the life of faith. Reach out to those who are shaky in their faith.

Jude 24–25. This passage is one of the most beautiful prayers in the Bible.

REVELATION

OVERVIEW

- *Revelation in a Nutshell. Revelation presents*
- *a broad, sweeping portrait of future events in*
- *order to strengthen the church, urge endur-*
- *ance in the face of trials, and encourage suf-*
- *fering believers. John was not merely trying*
- *to satisfy curiosity about the future; he*
- *wanted to instill moral earnestness among*
- *his readers. He wrote to urge his readers to*
- *obey the word of his prophecy.*

The structure of the book of Revelation is unique, grouping the message as it does in terms of the number seven. After the introduction (1:1–20), John addressed letters to seven churches (2:1–3:22). Next is the vision of heavenly worship (4:1–5:14).

Revelation 1:1–4. This revelation of Jesus Christ is conveyed to John through an angel. The purpose of the revelation is encouragement. It comes with a blessing to those who read and hear the prophecy and those who act on it.

Revelation 1:9–20. John had been exiled to Patmos, an island in the Mediterranean. There on a Lord's Day, the exalted Christ appeared to him and commanded him to write to the seven churches in Asia.

Revelation 2–3. Most of these seven letters contain words of both praise and correction.

Revelation 4–5. The scene changes. The setting is heaven. John described the throne of God

Background. According to early Christian traditions, the Gospel of John, the three Epistles of John, and Revelation were all written by the Apostle John. Revelation is the only one of these books that actually claimed to be written by someone named John. The author did not claim to be the Apostle John. Given the authority and prestige of the Twelve, no other first-century Christian leader was associated closely enough with the churches of Asia Minor to have spoken so authoritatively and to have referred to himself simply as John unless he were, in fact, the Apostle.

"Thou art worthy, O Lord to receive glory and honor and power: for thou hast created all things, and for thy pleasure they are and were created" (Rev. 4:11, KJV).

surrounded by the company of heaven continually praising God. God took a scroll with seven seals on it. An angel asks who is worthy to open the scroll by breaking the seals. At first, no one is found. John began to weep. Then one of the elders around the throne said that the Lion of Judah is worthy to break the seals. This Lion is none other than the Lamb who took the scroll out of God's right hand. At that, those surrounding the throne broke into a new song praising and worshiping the Lamb.

Revelation 6:1–8:5. The first four seals represent judgments of God on the earth: military aggression, war, famine, and death. The fifth seal reveals the martyrs in heaven and their appeal to God for justice. The sixth seal represents a shaking of the elements of nature and all of the consequences of that for human life. Between the sixth and seventh seal, 144,000 of the tribes of Israel are given a seal of protection on their foreheads. When the seventh seal is opened, there is silence in heaven for half an hour, and seven angels are given trumpets.

Revelation 8:6–11:19. The first four of the angels blow their trumpets, announcing judgments on the earth: destruction of plants, marine life, fresh water, and the heavenly bodies. The sixth trumpet heralds a plague of locusts. The seventh trumpet blows, and one-third of human beings are killed. A mighty angel descended to earth with a small scroll in his hand. He commanded John to eat the scroll. At first, the scroll tasted sweet, but then it turned sour in his stomach. The angel told John that he must prophesy. After an interlude, the seventh trumpet is blown, indicating the beginning of the end.

Revelation 12–14. The dragon (Satan) seeks to destroy the woman (God's people) and her offspring (Christ). Two beasts, one from the sea and another from the earth, deceive many by their power and miracles. John then witnessed the consequences of being deceived by the beasts.

Revelation 15–16. Seven bowls of God's wrath are poured out on the earth.

Revelation 17–18. Babylon (the Roman Empire) is overthrown.

Revelation 19. The rider on a white horse leads the charge against the beast and false prophet who are thrown into a lake of fire.

Revelation 20. An angel throws Satan into the Abyss where he is kept for a thousand years, during which time Christ rules on earth. After the thousand years, Satan is released and makes one last stand against God. Satan is then thrown into the lake of fire into which the beast and false prophet had been thrown.

Revelation 21–22. The new heaven and earth appear. One last invitation is given to come and drink the water of life.

THEOLOGICAL INSIGHTS

The book of Revelation shows theological richness despite its complex symbolism. The book represents crucial doctrinal insights for God's people. These center on many major doctrinal teachings, some of which are:

God's Sovereignty. The entire book repeatedly witnesses to God's sovereignty over all human history, activities, and institutions. Neither Satan nor his representations in human rulers or religious leaders can overcome God's purposes. In fact, God works out His purposes even through their evil (17:17). The sovereignty of God is the foundation for hope and the promise of victory in the midst of persecution and suffering.

Jesus Christ. Jesus Christ is the book's central figure. He gave the revelation (1:1) and is the only One able to clarify history's meaning by opening the mysterious scroll (5:5). He is worthy to do so because of His redemptive death and resurrection (5:5–14). He is closely identified with God's Spirit (5:6–7) and is Israel's expected Messiah or Christ (v. 5). He is divine, worthy to receive the glory due to God (5:12). The theme of Revelation is the ultimate victory of Christ in His Second Coming (1:7; 19:11–21; 22:7, 12, 17, 20). He will establish God's kingdom in which He and the Father will rule with the saints (21:1–22:5). He will reign in the millennium (20:4), and He will marry His bride, the church, eternally (19:7–9).

The Holy Spirit. References to the Holy Spirit provide the basis for a doctrine of the Trinity. Individual believers have the Spirit's presence (1:10). The Spirit speaks a word of hope to the churches (2:7, 11, 17, 29; 3:6, 13, 22; 14:13). The Spirit was an agent in revealing Holy Scripture to John (21:10) and is active in calling for Christ's return and for people to come to Christ (22:17).

Christ's Kingdom. Christ's kingdom is presented both as His eternal rule and as His present rule over His churches (Rev. 2–3). The church represents God's people of the New Covenant in historical existence. Locally, individual churches exist (1:4; 2:1–3:22). Christ is the Head of the church and has authority over it (2:1). The local church teaches good doctrine and disciplines false teachers (2:2–23), proclaims and testifies to the gospel in evangelistic missionary outreach (2:13), and supports other churches.

The Believer's Response to God's Rule. The picture of the kingdom shows how God's saints respond to His rule: with singing, service, and praise (5:9–13; 7:4–17; 14:2–3; 15:2–4; 19:6). Suffering saints on earth can count on the power of their prayers to the heavenly King on His throne (8:3–5). At the end time Christ's kingdom will be consummated in all its glory, and His reign will be absolute (11:15–19). Christ's kingdom is the goal toward which Christian hope is aimed.

Heaven. The glories of heaven are beyond human imagination. God's presence permeates all of heaven (21:22). Absolutely no evil will be there (21:27; 22:3). Believers can be certain of entering heaven, for our names are written in the book of life (3:5). The Lamb marks His own (22:4). The certainty of heaven does not eliminate the need to urge faithfulness, for a call to faithfulness permeates Revelation.

Hell. Those not in the book of life face eternal punishment or hell. This is described as the bottomless pit or Abyss (9:2; 11:7; 17:8; 20:3), the home of demons, evil spirits, and the eternally dead. It is where the satanic beast comes from (13:11). It is a place of eternal torment (14:10–11; 19:3, 20; 20:10, 15; 21:8). Hell is the result of judgment on evil and evil ones, a consequence of Christ's victory over evil and His bringing justice for His saints (16:5–7).

Sin. Sin appears in many forms in the world: sexual sins (9:21; 21:8; 22:15), worship of false

"And I saw the dead, the great and the small, standing before the throne, and the books were opened; and another book was opened, which is the book of life; and the dead were judged from the things which were written in the books, according to their deeds" (Rev. 20:12, NASB).

gods (9:20; 13:4, 8, 14–16; 14:11; 21:8; 22:15), involvement in the occult (9:20–21; 18:23; 21:8; 22:15), murder (9:21; 21:8; 22:15), theft (9:21), killing believers (17:6; 18:24), slave trading (18:13), lying (21:27; 22:15), economic sins (18:3, 11–19), political sins (17:2, 4, 7–13), and cowardice (21:8), which probably refers to those who professed the faith but did not endure. Basically, sin in Revelation is trust in the satanic forces of political and false religious leaders rather than trust in the King of kings.

Satan. Satan is clearly depicted as the author of sin. He has the key to the Abyss (9:1–2). He attacks God's witnesses (11:7–10). He sought to destroy Christ (12:1–6) but lost the battle (12:7–11). Ever since that time, he has feverishly attacked Christ's disciples (12:12–13:1). He will marshal forces against God (16:13–14; 19:19) but will be defeated (19:20–21). Christ will bind them in the Abyss (20:1–3), but Satan will gain freedom and again attack God but without success (20:7–10).

Humanity. Revelation shows an understanding of the destructive capabilities of humanity as well as the evil of Satan. Some humans respond to God's grace and are saved, faithfully serving God (6:9–11), while others obstinately refuse to repent (9:20–21; 16:8–11). Clearly, perseverance is a clear indicator of genuine faith (1:9; 22:7). Satan attacks believers constantly (12:17), requiring believers to remain faithful (1:3; 13:10; 14:12; 21:7; 22:14). True faithfulness is displayed through sincere worship of God and obedience to His standard of moral purity (14:3–5).

Personal Holiness. The strength to remain faithful rests on a special type of relationship with

God through Christ known as the priesthood of all believers (1:6; 5:10). God revealed His covenant identity to His people on Sinai (Exod. 19:6). Revelation affirms this identity for the church. All citizens of God's kingdom, not just political or religious officials, are to mediate God's salvation to the nations, approach God for themselves, and accept responsibility for personal holiness before God.

The Bible. The book of Revelation shows us important points in teaching about the Bible. Revelation is a direct product of Jesus' revealing His word to John (Rev. 1:1). It was written down immediately (1:10–11). He did not receive permission to write everything he heard (10:2–4). The writing had a definite purpose (1:1) and was expected to be read and obeyed (1:3; 22:9–10). The trustworthiness of the Revelation is asserted (22:6). Its authority is recognized immediately, so that nothing should be added or taken away (22:18–19). The inspired book had words of immediate application to specific congregations (2:1–3:22), has continuing meaning, and has an end-time meaning.

Angels. Angels appear more frequently in Revelation than in most biblical books. Each church has an angel (1:20), but the exact interpretation here is disputed: pastors, guardian angel, or heavenly counterpart of the earthly church. Angels serve as heavenly heralds (5:2) and heavenly messengers on earth to protect God's people (7:1–3). Angels may have great authority (18:1), even holding the key to hell (20:1) and being able to introduce people to God's secrets (21:9–10). Still, angels are not to receive human worship (22:8–9). They worship God (5:11; 7:11). Some angels are not faithful to God, for they follow Satan (12:7–9).

"I testify to everyone who hears the words of prophecy of this book: if anyone adds to them, God shall add to him the plagues which are written in this book; and if anyone takes away from the words of the book of this prophecy, God shall take away his part from the tree of life and from the holy city, which are written in this book."
(Rev. 22:18–19, NASB).

"The Spirit and the bride say, 'Come!' And let him who hears say, 'Come!' Whoever is thirsty, let him come; and whoever wishes, let him take the free gift of the water of life" (Rev. 22:17).

Christ's Final Victory. Essentially, Revelation is about history; it reveals its meaning and reveals Christ's final victory at its end. Caesar and Rome appeared to control history rather than God controlling it, but He will be ultimately victorious. God's kingdom will be established. The suffering of God's people will be avenged. The satanic forces will suffer eternally. Jesus is coming.

The following list is a collection of the resources used for this volume. All are from Broadman & Holman's list of published reference resources. All of these works will greatly aid in the reader's study, teaching, and presentation of the truths of the New Testament. The accompanying annotations can be helpful in guiding the reader to the proper resources.

RESOURCES

Adams, J. McKee, Rev. by Joseph A. Callaway. *Biblical Backgrounds*. This work provides valuable information on physical and geographical settings. Its many colorful maps and other features add depth and understanding.

Blair, Joe. *Introducing the New Testament*. A high-level overview that contains outlines of books, special graphics, maps and photos, and summary questions.

Holman Bible Dictionary. An exhaustive, alphabetically arranged resource of Bible-related subjects. An excellent tool of definitions and other information on the people, places, things, and events.

Holman Bible Handbook. A comprehensive treatment that offers outlines, commentary on key themes, sections and full-color photos, illustrations, charts, and maps. Provides an accent on broader theological teachings.

Holman Book of Biblical Charts, Maps, and Reconstructions. A colorful, visual collection of charts, maps, and reconstructions. These well-designed tools are invaluable to Bible study.

Lea, Thomas D. *The New Testament: Its Background and Message*. An excellent resource for background material—political, cultural, his-

torical, and religious. Provides background information in broad
strokes on specific books, including the Gospels.

The *New American Commentary*. Volumes available: Matthew, Mark,
Luke, John 1–11, Acts, Romans, 2 Corinthians, Galatians, Ephesians,
Philippians-Colossians-Philemon, 1, 2 Timothy-Titus, and James.